Dear Donald, Dear Bennett

RANDOM HOUSE

NEW YORK

Dear Donald, Dear Bennett

THE WARTIME CORRESPONDENCE OF
BENNETT CERF AND DONALD KLOPFER

Bennett Cerf and Donald Klopfer

INTRODUCTION BY BOB LOOMIS

Library of Congress Cataloging-in-Publication Data
Cerf, Bennett, 1898–1971.
Dear Donald, Dear Bennett: the wartime correspondence of Bennett Cerf and
Donald Klopfer/Bennett Cerf and Donald Klopfer; introduction by
Bob Loomis.—1st ed.
p.   cm.
ISBN 0-375-50768-X (acid-free paper)
1. Cerf, Bennett, 1898–1971—Correspondence. 2. Klopfer, Donald,
1902–1986—Correspondence. 3. Publishers and publishing—United
States—Correspondence. 4. Random House (Firm)—History. 5. World War,
1939–1945—Personal narratives, American. I. Klopfer, Donald, 1902–1986.
II. Title.
Z473.C45 C47 2002
070.5'092—dc21   2001048382

Printed in the United States of America on acid-free paper
Random House website address: www.atrandom.com

24689753

FIRST EDITION

Book design by Carole Lowenstein

My lucky star is a house—and an imaginary one at that. Rockwell Kent drew it, one day, sitting in my office, and it was adopted forthwith as a trade mark for our publishing firm. We called it Random House because we said we were going to publish anything under the sun that came along—if we liked it well enough. That was in 1928. We're trying to make the star burn a little brighter each year.

Bennett Cerf

Introduction

In 1942, Bennett Cerf and Donald Klopfer had been inseparable partners for fifteen years, ever since they founded Random House in 1927. Neither Bennett, who was forty-three, nor Donald, who was forty, was eligible for the draft. At first glance, if asked which of the two was more likely to take a leave from Random House and volunteer to fight in World War II, anyone would of course have said Bennett.

But it was Donald who enlisted in the United States Army Air Forces. Bennett must have been taken aback, even envious I think, when Donald announced he was joining up. It was more than a desire, as far as Donald was concerned, it was a duty—and you had to know him to understand just how morally strong that feeling was.

Donald was the rock of Random House. He had a deep affection and respect for books and the people who made them. He was the sort of person whose simple presence could help you solve your problems. He believed publishers had a special obligation; he once told a writer whose politics he disagreed with that he would publish his book if no one else would. When we gave a dinner for Ayn Rand at the publication of *Atlas Shrugged* one of her minions announced ahead of time that everyone from Random House was to toast her and that she would then judge each person's loyalty to her. "Of course," this minion said, "Mr. Klopfer doesn't have to give a toast if he doesn't want to. He's a gentleman."

Bennett was a perfect complement to Donald, but there were never two people who were so close yet so different. Bennett loved life—Bill Styron called him "a life-giver" at his funeral.

He loved publishing, authors, and publicity. Everything about books excited him—as these letters so delightfully demonstrate. His eagerness and openness made him a perfect target for practical jokes—and this was strangely endearing. Tony Wimpfheimer, who was the managing editor, had once had the first few copies of Bennett's newest joke book bound upside down, and then we waited for Bennett to come screaming down the hall to his office. Another time Lew Miller, our sales manager, dressed up in a fake mustache, goatee, and a suit from central casting and was ushered into Bennett's office by Bob Haas, who introduced him as the French author of a novel we had just published. Bob tried to keep a straight face as he translated "gentleman Lew's" Fractured French. Bennett was bug-eyed when Lew pulled off his mustache—but he laughed as hard as they did. Once one of these jokes backfired. Chris, Bennett's son, sheepishly entered Bennett's office one Monday morning and confessed that he had gotten married over the weekend. He showed his father Polaroid wedding pictures. Bennett was dumbfounded, and then he burst into tears.

The only thing I can think of that Bennett disliked was meetings. If he walked into a room with more than two people he would turn around and leave.

Bennett and Donald saw Random House pretty much as a big family, and they acted accordingly. If someone needed help they were there. They once tried to tell a senior editor that while he could remain as long as he wanted to he might be happier if he found a job elsewhere. The editor said he was under a lot of strain because he wasn't able to buy a house in New Jersey that his wife wanted. Bennett and Donald immediately loaned him the money. The same thing happened to me, though I said nothing at all to them about wanting to buy a co-op that I couldn't afford. Out of the blue they called me into Bennett's office and Donald wrote out a personal check and handed it to me. I'd been at Random House only six months. One morning Bennett came to work and found our sterling receptionist—Debbie DeBanzie—crying. Bennett stopped and asked her what was the matter. She showed him a letter from RCA that congratulated her on her retirement. Sobbing, she said she wasn't able to go back to Scotland yet. Bennett immediately told her that she could sit there as long as she wanted and from then on he would personally pay her salary, and he did.

Donald went to England as an intelligence officer in the 445th Bomb Group, and in his V-mail he modestly related his adventures to Bennett as well as his concern for Random House and even his future there. Bennett in turn wrote fully and faithfully—and with an exuberance unique to him—everything that was happening in the world of books.

As a result we are now the beneficiaries of these wonderful letters. I believe there is nothing quite like them. Not only are they a unique window into publishing, but they portray a perfect partnership. It was almost as though they were born to be together, so perfectly did they fit. The two men had a remarkable affection for one another. I've never known two men who were so genuinely close and respected each other with such intensity.

Their correspondence flourished, at times almost daily, for two and one half years, a test for any relationship. Many more letters passed between them than are printed here. A few of the letters have been edited where they were repetitious or dealt with personal matters, real estate, insurance, or taxes. Most people who worked at Random House have been identified, but not all of the hundreds of people Bennett and Donald otherwise encountered.

—*Bob Loomis*

Note to the Reader

We have duplicated Bennett's block paragraph style and use of uppercasing book titles in his typewritten correspondence to Donald exactly per original letters. The letters of Donald to Bennett, on the other hand, were mostly handwritten, and we have retained his indented paragraphs and informal, upper/lowercase style of treating book titles.

1942

WESTERN UNION

BENNETT CERF=
1942 JUN 2 PM 7 41
                20 EAST 57 ST NYK=
MY ADDRESS FOR THIRTY DAYS WILL BE AVIATION
CADET SECTION SAAAB SANTAANA CALIF GOOD
LUCK LOVE=
                DONALD.

MACKAY RADIO POSTAL TELEGRAPH

June 3, 1942

CAPTAIN DONALD S. KLOPFER
AVIATION CADET SECTION
S.A.A.A.B.
SANTA ANA, CALIF.

DELIGHTED TO HEAR FROM YOU. PAT* RELAYED
YOUR PHONE CONVERSATION. OFFICE SEEMS EMPTY
WITHOUT YOU BUT WILL HOLD OUT IF JEZE-

*Pat Klopfer, Donald's wife.

BELS* OLD NUMBER EIGHTY EIGHT DOES. BUSINESS BECAME TERRIFIC MOMENT YOU LEFT. THIRTEEN HUNDRED PARIS [*The Last Time I Saw Paris* by Elliot Paul] SO FAR THIS WEEK NOT TO MENTION THREE HUNDRED GREEK DRAMA AND FIVE HUNDRED TACITUS. FROM COLUMBIA. LOVE AND KISSES

June 9, 1942

Dear Klopf:

Harry Maule has just started to give the plot of the new Mignon Eberhart book to the electrified sales conference, so I ought to have about an hour and a half of free time to clean up the mess on the desk and finally get off a letter to you. As you can imagine, I have been literally up to my neck ever since you left getting jacket dummies, and what not ready for the conference. It has gone wonderfully and I see a little daylight ahead.

Under separate cover, I am sending you copies of the summer list, the juvenile list, and the multigraphed fall list. It was the last job that was the tough one, of course, but I don't think that the result is bad.

Bob Linscott came down yesterday [from Houghton Mifflin, where he was still employed, though he was about to agree to come to RH] to sit in on the conference and was literally overwhelmed by the wealth of stuff we've got on this fall program.

---

*Nickname of Pauline Kreiswirth, secretary to Cerf and Klopfer.

Barring unforeseen transportation difficulties and the like, we really ought to clean up in the coming six months and that should be a happy thought for you while you are learning to do right shoulder arms. Incidentally, I am the only man in the history of the U.S. Army who ever cut his nose while performing this simple manual. I did it with the sight on my gun and won the official title for my squad of "The Bloody Fifth."

Everybody in the office was delighted with your two letters. We all envy you the experience that you are having and I am particularly sad that I can't be with you every morning to get up at 6 o'clock. You know how I always love to breathe in the early morning air.

Bob* and Saxe† I know, have written you all the detailed news of the office. The total on PARIS last week was over 2500 copies. The coming Sunday Tribune tabulations are a clear first with 60 points; *Cross Creek* [Marjory Kinnon Rawlings] is back in second place with 52. The Benson book [Sally Benson, *Junior Miss*] isn't going to set any worlds on fire, but on the other hand, it will be a comfortable success. Yesterday's total was 166 copies for it. I think we'll surely hit 8000 and very possibly ten. The big surprise for us this summer may well be Quentin Reynolds' ONLY THE STARS ARE NEUTRAL. We are beginning to get enthusiastic telegrams from several accounts and Kroch [owner of a Chicago bookstore], my new-found buddy, wired to increase his order from 25 copies to 100. The first review I have seen is a proof of Linton Wells' review for the Saturday Review of Literature. It is an unqualified rave. This book really may go places.

*Robert K. Haas, partner.
†Saxe Commins, senior editor.

. . .

We haven't lifted a finger to get any of the boys who came home on the Drottningholm. Denney and Loechner are the only two who seem to have any story to tell, and they seem to be spilling the works in their syndicated newspaper articles. I guess we are the only publishers in America who haven't gone after them. Herb Matthews was in to see us. He isn't a bit sore about the Spanish book. He thinks he has a good book in him on the Italian business, but is honest enough to say he doesn't think he will have time to write it before he is off again, this time for India. The Times saved this post for him for months. Most of the other boys who came home on the Drottningholm haven't the faintest idea of the kind of work they are going to find from now on.

I sat up until almost 3 o'clock this morning galloping through Sam Adams' THE HARVEY GIRLS. It is really a pretty good yarn, but shows the effect of a rush job. I think we can safely count on selling about 6000 of it. Bernice* is going to try to sell it as a one-shot to Cosmopolitan, in which event we'll get 10% of those proceeds. We are also in for 10% of the movie price (excepting the $5000.00 down payment) and, since I understand that MGM like the job that Adams has done, we may get quite a substantial sum out of this end of the project, too.

Mannie†, Abe‡ and I had a fine old time with your inventory job the other afternoon. The final figure will be about 3800. The Duplaix stuff is figured at 13¢. The Modern Library figure isn't what it used to be. I'd like to give you more complete details.

---

*Bernice Baumgarten, subsidiary rights.
†Emanuel E. Harper, assistant secretary and treasurer.
‡Abe Friedman.

Before I do so, I wish you'd tell me how many other people are likely to see our letters to you—if any!

Everybody in the office misses you like hell. Your manicure girl informed me this morning that she managed to get a kiss in before she left. You've been holding out on me, Klopfer.

The only item of social interest concerns the party at Bob's tomorrow afternoon. I understand that a big exhibition doubles match has been arranged involving Haas and Kreiswirth on one side and Mrs. Haas and Cerf on the other. Bets are flowing freely. I think we ought to win because I am thoroughly hep to Jezebel's weaknesses. Incidentally, I hope my wire to you came through in ungarbled form and that you remembered the title of our old No. 88! [*Flowering Judas*, Katherine Anne Porter]

I realize that you are working your whoosises off, but please remember that we are all terribly anxious to hear as full reports of your activities as you can possibly give us. Your letters are passed from hand to hand and literally devoured by everybody in the place.

Let me know if there is anything at all I can do for you here. And please tell your Commanding Officer that we would like to have you stationed permanently at Governor's Island as soon as your training course is over. If Cerf's recommendation won't do this, maybe I can get a letter from Major Silberberg (boy, could I have spit when I heard this bit of news!). Incidentally, I will probably have the pleasure of seeing that old shit (I had to spell this word out to Jezebel, she had never heard it) on Thursday afternoon.

Do you want PW [*Publishers Weekly*] or any other things of that sort sent to you? Or would you rather not be bothered with trade details so that you can keep your mind clear for military matters?

As ever,
Bennett

June 9/42

Dear Bennett—

Had a week-end of dissipation, my last day off this month, I've been told. Saturday night I took the bus up to Beverly Hills to Edgar.* Spent the night there and found the Selwyn family en masse. Billy looks like an ugly Quent Reynolds! Sunday Georgie came over, we went to Lee and Ira's [Gershwin's brother] for a drink. Saw Alex Aarons, Irwin Shaw and some others and then to supper at Artie Schwartz's, Knopfs,† Leonard Lees and others there. It seemed a little like wandering into "21," everyone was there and everyone sends love to you. Little Annie has evidently given Georgie the brush off and he can't understand it. I just cannot disillusion him if he hasn't enough sense yet!

This army business is still lots of fun. In four weeks they effect to make experts out of us in Chemical Warfare, High Altitude Flying, Mess Management, Close order Drill and everything else having to do with the Army Air Forces. It will give us a good birds-eye picture of the whole thing. That will be wonderful to have no matter what work I finally do.

The routine is pretty much the same—up at 6-15 in the

---

*Edgar Selwyn, Pat's uncle.
†Alfred's brother Edwin and wife.

morning, working all day at drill and lectures, a little studying at night and turning in pretty early as I'm usually dead by dinner time. It wouldn't be so hard if I were living at the Base but there are no married men there—and they just haven't the accommodations. It's fascinating to watch this camp grow. It opened Feb. 15th. They now have about twelve thousand men here and before they're thru' it will be five times the size it is now. I've seen the final plans for it, and they're something. The officers are a good group of guys but I haven't made any real friends yet. I guess I'm too choosy, and we're all too busy!

I haven't read a line other than military stuff since I've gotten here—don't ever see the Times or Trib— Has Paris gotten to 1st place yet! And what's happening in N.Y. I haven't heard a word from you—you bastard.

Give my love to Thrup* and Jezebel—and a good pinch for Christopher† from his Uncle Donald.

Take care of yourself and don't work too hard. I'm mighty lonesome for 20 East.—

My love, as always—
Donald

June, 1942

Dear Bennett:

I haven't written for the past week because unfortunately I broke the middle finger of my right hand, thereby causing me considerable inconvenience, and I am sure causing you consid-

---

*Phyllis Cerf, Bennett's wife (after thrupence, the smallest English coin).
†Christopher Cerf, Bennett and Phyllis's son.

erable laughter. I have been working hard all week long and have gotten letters from Saxe and Mannie, but nothing from you. How about keeping me posted as to what's happening in our dear office. I realize you are as busy as the very devil but work Pauline overtime just about once a week, so I know what the devil is happening. If I am permanently stationed here I will want PW sent to me as I certainly want to keep in touch to see what's happening in the world of books. Frankly, I haven't much time to read but I don't want to get out of touch. Will you please send me, charging my account, six copies of "Attack" as soon as they're off the press? I think I can use them to good advantage out here.

Thank Phyllis for the pictures that she sent me. I think they're wonderful and I'll write to her as soon as I am able to. This letter is short and with no information, but I'll be back on the ball by the end of the week.

Give my love to everyone in the office.

As always,
Donald

June 16, 1942

Dear Don:

We are all terribly sorry to hear about your busted digit, but I suppose that sort of thing is inevitable when they blast ausgespielte old poops out of their easy chairs and put them into competition once more with active young bucks like myself. I hope you haven't been too inconvenienced by the mishap. It is hard to realize that you are over 60% finished with your training course already; as you know, you are squeezing more into each week than happens here at the old bailiwick in six months—and I envy you a little bit more every day.

News from Random House is all good. PARIS keeps romping along. The total for last week was about 2000. Yesterday 600 more and, in the first mail this morning, there was an order of 500 from the News Company and 250 from the Book-of-the-Month Club. I guess we are up to about 33,000 now and, from present indications, we ought to hit 50,000 before we are finished.

Sally's book is moving too at the rate of between 100 and 250 a day. Macy's Modern Library order yesterday was for 2800 of the regulars—about the biggest Modern Library order we've gotten from that bailiwick in many a long day. I am still trying to get them to use the THREE FAMOUS SPY NOVELS for their July mystery book of the month. Peg [Macy's book buyer] and George are coming up to my house for dinner on Monday night, along with the Hollisters, the Farnols and the Ernie Heyns. For your information, Ernie Heyn is the new editor-in-chief of Liberty Magazine, and I am trying to sell him PARIS as a one-shot condensation. You will recall the new Mrs. Ernie Heyn when I tell you that her name was once Ethel Butter-worth!

First reviews on Quent's book are out and out raves. Kroch has gone crazy about it and sent letters to all his customers saying that it is the most exciting book he has read in 35 years. I wouldn't be surprised if we went over 10,000 on this one. All in all, I feel like sending a telegram of congratulation to Mr. Morgenthau.

As I indicated to you, we are going to show a profit of about $3800.00. The preliminary figure is $145,000.00. We wrote all the dollar Whitman stuff down to 13¢ and all the Lifetime Library Books down to 40¢ and 50¢ apiece. This accounted for a great deal, but we still had to drop the price of all the Modern Library books, including the Giants, about 3¢ apiece in order to get the desired results. I honestly think that there will be no question about this because, even at the new figure, our Modern Library inventory is still way higher than it was a year ago and is so big that we feel fully justified in marking it down et al, and our stock will be as clean as a bone in a few days' time. And by God, we mean to keep it that way. After this we are going to let books go out of print when the demand starts dribbling off rather than getting ourselves stuck with a whole new edition. This has happened all too frequently in the past. We are all watching this stock problem together now. In fact, the team work has been marvelous and if only we don't lose more key people in the course of the coming weeks we'll get along O.K. I am afraid Russell* and Whitney will be the next to go.

Last night about 150 people gathered at the Ambassador for a surprise dinner to Amy Loveman. It really turned out to be a wonderful affair. Elmer Davis spoke just before hopping off to his new job in Washington. Chris Morley and Tom Lamont also gave amusing talks. The voice of the publishing industry also made a magnificent impression, but modesty forbids me to go into further detail in this connection. Bob Linscott and Bob Haas occupied the guest room at 132 after the party was over. Tonight Merle and Bob, Charlie Addams and Boris Karloff are coming to the house for dinner. That is about the sum total of my social life for the month.

It looks as though Doubleday Doran have managed to get rid of their Garden City plant to the Perry Gyroscope Company. The

---

*Jim Russell, RH salesman.

deal hasn't gone through yet, but Wolff and Satenstein are sitting around licking their chops in gleeful anticipation of new business. The deal won't hurt that rickety Doubleday balance sheet, however! Gene Reynal is off for the Navy and Reed has gotten a job with Curtise Hitchcock. Speaking of Satenstein, I read THE LAST MAN COMES HOME over the weekend. I am sorry to report that it is probably the worst piece of garbage that we ever brought out under the Random House imprint. We are going to print 5000 copies from type and let it go at that.

Oh hell, that's enough for now. Go back to your drill and remember that we all love you and miss you here. I wish I were coming over with Pat tomorrow!

As ever,
Bennett

June 18/1942

Dear Bennett:

I never did receive the various lists you promised me. Tell Pauline to send me the summer list and the mimeographical sheet! She's neglecting me horribly—but I suspect you're keeping her busy, and I'm forgotten.

As you can see by this letter my finger is out of its splint and I can't bend it much yet but on the whole it didn't bother me too much. They marched the ass off us to-day and then put us thru' gas chambers so that we were tear gassed—then I found out a gas mask really works. This week has been dryer (I hope you spell it that way) than heretofore—we're having a lot of

military law and company management—last night I was assistant Officer of the Day—stayed up all night—posted guards.
Ran around the grounds in a car—acted important all around
and got mighty tired. Week after next I know what they'll do
with me—for a few weeks anyway—but not for much more
than that.

I am mighty depressed by the Libyan news. But here you
can't tell anything—but it doesn't look good to me. Maybe I'll
get to India yet.

Give my love to the gang—I can't write all of them
separately—but I certainly miss that bunch—they're swell and
I'm lonesome for them and especially you—you old horse.

Congratulations on the May deal—no Book Club choice?

> Love,
> Donald

June 19, 1942

Dear Donald:

You've got a hell of a chutzpah kicking about my lack of writing when poor little Jezebel typed her fingers to the bone the
other night on a document that was three paragraphs longer
than WAR AND PEACE. And we don't want to hear any crap
about letters crossing in the mail either!

By the time this letter reaches you Pat will already have told
you all the social news. Here is the business dope in a nutshell.

Good old Moriarty died on Wednesday night. I am sure you
will feel just as badly about it as I did. Paul Rossiter took care of

sending flowers for us. Paul will probably get the job at the Coop [Yale].

Our old friend Zevin reports that BATTLE FOR ASIA will probably be a very big seller for them. He is making it his headline feature for the fall. While he was in a good mood about all this I sold him LAST MAN AROUND THE WORLD. He is coming up this afternoon to sign the contract and, by that time, I hope to find something else around that I can unload upon him.

Harry Maule says the new Maritta Wolff book has terrific possibilities. I won't read it until he has cut it down a couple of hundred pages or so.

You will get six copies of ATTACK just as soon as they are ready. Looks like we may have something really big in that book.

We have decided to give PARIS a shot in the arm by trying out one of those 10% free book promotions. The first day's response was orders for 1000 each from Baker and the News Company, and 250 from Macy. Zowie.

ONLY THE STARS ARE NEUTRAL is off to a really good start and the Benson is moving too. The enclosed ad should knock you for a loop. Sally, incidentally, was in to see me yesterday for the first time since her return and was all friendship and cream puffs. She never even mentioned the mixup over the play edition of JUNIOR MISS.

I hear that Graystone is footch. I also hear that the Doubleday plan for selling the plant to Sperry has hit a snag and is likely to fall through.

. . .

Gene Reynal got into the Navy and leaves in a few weeks. Mait Edey has just gotten his commission as Second Lieutenant in the Air Force and is off for Biloxi, Miss.

The eyes of the sporting world are on Rips 54th Street Tennis Court, where at 5 o'clock this afternoon the extremely nebich combination of Commins and Kreiswirth will undoubtedly be crushed under the smashing volleys of Mr. and Mrs. Bennett A. Cerf.

Fred Melcher gave a luncheon yesterday for about 60 publishers to enlarge your old War Council. Mention was made of the fact that you were off in the army. The vote to enlarge the work of the committee was a 64 to 1 in favor. I need hardly tell you that the guy who voted nay very loudly was old Alfie Knopf. He said he thought the whole business was a God damn waste of time. Between ourselves, I have a hunch that Alfie's got something there!

Leah Daniels has decided to retire and be a housewife. I am trying to persuade Frances Merriam to take the job. I will let you know more about this next week.

I guess that's about all. All of us are working like hell, but it seems to agree with us.

Love,
Bennett

June 23, 1942

Dear Cerfie—

Klopfer has been assigned for two days to Squadron 47, 180 nice little pilot cadets, and promptly was made O.D. here. He had just taken his little boys to mess and about to see that they are nicely tucked in, but at 10 o'clock. What a grand bunch of youngsters they are. If I can't get a good job in Intelligence I am almost hoping to be a Squadron Commander with these cadets. They're really right out of the top drawer, most of them from the Middle West, very young, very eager and quite intelligent. It might be fun wet nursing them thru' their preliminary training. But I forgot I'm back in the work business. They're doing a 600 page training manual out here and want it privately printed so Klopfer has been called in as an expert, and in comparison with these dopes I am. But I don't want to be thrown into that job completely. I'd still like to go to Harrisburg but I'll know my next assignment Monday as I'm out of school this Saturday. Expect a beautifully engraved diploma. This week I've been alternately getting printing quotations from Los Angeles and pulling a Colt 45 apart. I can get it apart but there are usually a few parts left over when I put it together. Wait until I get at a machine gun.

If the British pull many more Tobrucks I'll really see active service. I can't understand it and I can't believe there's any valid cause. By the time you receive this I'm sure Savestopol will have fallen and then the trouble will really begin.

Thanks so much for all the business information. How about a little of the bad news. Things can't be going as well as you insinuate. Have they been throwing many Victory Marches back? How's the old cash position? Will they ever sell enough books to pay off that loan? And tell Abe to send me the monthly statements. I'm really not complaining Cerfie, I'm just lonesome for the life I've led for 17 years, the language I've spoken in that time and the friends that are so dear to me.

Pat and Tony* arrived safely. We're living in a little apartment in Laguna Beach. Mrs. K. is doing the cooking and
damned well, too, and, when I get home, it's very nice. . . .

I'm having a lot of fun here but it doesn't look as tho' I'll get
to India with a Combat Squadron. Fix it for me, please.

My love to all Bob, Saxe, Lew—my beautiful Pauline—and
all and family. Kiss Phyllis and Chris for me.

Love,
Donald

Who'll replace Leah [Gadlow] and the youngsters upstairs?

June 23, 1942

Dear Klopf:

Stung by the derisive concluding sentence of your last letter,
"no book club choice?" I swung my 88mm guns yesterday at
Harry Scherman, Meredith Wood and Harry Abrams, and
think I've got them reasonably well sold on the use of THE
WISDOM OF CHINA AND INDIA for a future book dividend. They fished out their own records on the sale of the little
Confucius volume in the Modern Library and, when they saw
that it was exceeded only by OF HUMAN BONDAGE and A
FAREWELL TO ARMS, the flag of Random House began to
flap victoriously in the breeze. The deal isn't closed yet by a
hell of a long shot but, from now on, I will worry them into it if
I possibly can. My motto is "If a finger-breaking schlemiel like

*Charles A. Wimpfheimer, Klopfer's stepson.

Klopfer can sell them Proust, Cerf ought to be able to sell them the great thinkers of the Orient!" I will keep you posted.

Business continues very brisk on PARIS. It is still first in the Tribune surveys and we've crossed the 35,000 mark. In fact, it is safe to say we are pretty close to 40,000. Meanwhile, Quent's book is really off with a bang. Peggy Byrnes and George were at the house last night for dinner. Peg says it is selling faster at Macy's than any other book in the department at the moment. They sold 50 copies on Saturday and Monday! We are printing a new edition, bringing the total printed to 15,000, and the outlook couldn't be brighter. ST. LOUIS is over 7000 and still moving, but it hasn't got the zoom of the other two. CLARK GIFFORD is out today and I think it is absolutely hopeless, and I won't spend more than $100.00 in advertising. In fact, I may not spend a cent on it. The same goes for THUNDERBIRDS. We'll sell our 2000 copies (in addition to the 2000 to Fox) and forget about it. Bob is working hard on ATTACK and so is Saxe. We may have a real dark horse in this one.

The total May figures are as follows: M.L., $19044.43; M.L.G., $13074.80, R.H., $46,000 ($25,000 for June 1941).

The figures up to June 17th are: M.L. and M.L.G., $19,000 ($16,000 for June 1941); R.H., $46,000 ($25,000 for June 1941).

I wish we had more cash in the joint but, outside of that, everything is hunky dory and I really think that, with all of us watching the new printings like hawks, we are going to save an awful lot of money along this line in the months to come.

I am terribly anxious to hear what the future holds in store for you. Saturday will mark the close of your four-week period, and

I hope that you will soon know where you are booked for next. Please write the very minute you find out.

The news from Libya is certainly discouraging. John Gunther was at the house last night with Bubbles [Leonora Hornblow], but couldn't contribute any new facts for our enlightenment. Have I told you that Cecil Brown has landed the coveted five-minute news spot occupied by Elmer Davis? That won't hurt our book. Incidentally, the title of the Brown book has been changed to FROM SUEZ TO SINGAPORE. Do you like it?

I have been talking with Dan Longwell about that old plan for a Life book of war photographs. Wolff's estimate, however, for a 320 page book comes to about $1.10 a copy. To that we have to add a goodly sum for an editor and, all in all, the total investment would not be under $25,000.00. The Book-of-the-Month Club was very cold on the idea of using this book as a dividend and we have accordingly decided to turn the whole thing down flat. I am writing Longwell that we'll be interested when the war is actually over, but that if he wants to go ahead with one now, he will have to give it to another publisher. I am sure you will approve of this course.

The inter-office tennis matches on Friday produced some spirited competition. Thrup and I trimmed Jezebel and Saxe, but when Abe replaced Saxe we went down to inglorious defeat. Jez and Thrup looked magnificent on the court until a familiar-looking female began playing on the adjoining court. Her name was Alice Marble. Even Jezebel's incredible conceit collapsed in the face of a menace like this!

I hope that you've got a nice apartment at Laguna and that Pat is seeing enough of you to make her trip worth while. Write as often as you can and remember that everybody here loves you very much.

As ever,
Bennett

June 26, 1942

Dear Donald:

We were all deeply interested to hear that you are back at the old routine of getting printed quotations. My hunch is that you will turn out such a good job on this particular project that you will probably end up by producing the Congressional Record. After you have read a couple of issues of that, you will know something, my boy!

You ask for some of the bad business news along with the good. Honest Injun, Klopfer, there isn't any bad news at the moment except our cash position, which I presume is a reasonably familiar problem to you. At the present moment, we have accounts payable of $60,000, notes payable of $66,000. The latter figure includes $35,000 to the bank, $15,000 to ourselves and $16,000 in trade acceptances. Against that we have cash of only $11,000. The accounts receivable is between $130,000 and $140,000. This situation will probably get a little worse between now and September, but we are watching things very carefully and I don't think the adverse balance will grow alarmingly. From September on we really should right ourselves very quickly.

. . .

We are being absolutely ruthless about taking on new projects for next year. Every time I see the length of our Fall list, I froth at the mouth, but that is water under the bridge now and the only thing we can do is to really live up to our resolutions in the future. This I promise you faithfully will be done.

Very few of the VICTORY MARCH are bouncing back. It hasn't been a sensation anywhere, but everybody seems to realize that it is the time of year and not the book and they all are willing to string along until the Fall, when they think they will really go to town with the book. The sales chart shows 2463 copies for June up to the 22nd, making the total just a few hundred over the 50,000 mark. Under the circumstances, I think it is a great showing, and since we were smart enough not to reprint, we are sitting pretty. The June 22nd total on the card for PARIS is 34,000. This week will show about 3000 more. MEET ME IN ST. LOUIS is up to 7500 with about 400 added this week. ONLY THE STARS, by the end of this week, will be around the 10,000 mark. It will be 11th on the Tribune best seller chart week after this. PARIS falls to second on that chart, but it is a photo finish. On the second string, PAN AMERICAN SPANISH is rapidly approaching the 5000 mark. The first 22 days of June we sold 388 STORM, bringing the total up to 26,000. GREEK DRAMA is nudging the 15,000 mark (427 in the first three weeks of this month!). A CHILD'S BOOK OF PRAYERS goes on its merry way with over 600 this month and a total of almost 26,000. KEEPER OF THE FLAME is around 3300 and will probably die there. As you know, Grosset have this title for the Fall.

Zevin, as I think I told you, has taken LAST MAN AROUND THE WORLD and will probably add one or more other titles of ours later on. Doc Lewis [bookseller] has earmarked PRESCRIPTION FOR MURDER and AIR FORCE GIRL.

. . .

I am having Ernst Reichl design the whole WISDOM FOR CHINA AND INDIA and will have dummies to send to the Book-of-the-Month Club in about a week's time. We will also soon expect to get dummies of that JANE EYRE – WUTHERING HEIGHTS BOM dividend. We may be able to work out a special deal with Monroe Greenthal of United Artists on the Jane Eyre half of the dividend. That would be pure gravy, of course.

The final profit, after Martin Podoll got finished with his handiwork, was just over $2000.00. The terrific mark-off in inventory, a goodly part of which was absolutely necessary and not optional, shows where too much of our money has been going.

Georgie Opp called me up frantically at 2 o'clock this morning to tell me how anxious he is to get into some branch of service where, to quote him, he will be in danger. He says he'd like to have about twelve men under him and do a propaganda short somewhere in the firing line. It was all I could do to keep from laughing over the phone. George really is the world's greatest ass at times like this. I promised to speak to Lynn Farnol for him, but the mere thought of Oppenheimer in charge of a group of men at the front is enough to make me want to conclude a separate peace of my own with Japan.

John Gunther had a huge cocktail party the other day. Then a whole bunch of us spent an old-time New York night wandering the town. The tour included the Colony for dinner, the Barberry Room for drinks, and a final windup at "21." I should worry; the bills were all Gunther's, and I hate to think of what the total must have been. Included in the party were Bill Shirer, Bob Riskin, [Harold] Ross, Marc Connolly, [Samuel] Behrman, *Major* [Anatole] Litvak (!!!), Fay Wray, Jean Dalrymple, Howard Lindsay and his wife [Dorothy Stickney], and God knows who else. They came and went like ships in the night, if I may coin a phrase.

Two moves are on foot. One is to get Elmer Davis to do a 15-minute broadcast to the nation every week. I think this would be a wonderful idea and would do much to clarify the atmosphere. The second move involves a "Draft Willkie" campaign for the Governorship. I have agreed to do a little work on this project because I'd dearly love to see Mr. Dewey erased from the scene, and Willkie is obviously the only man who can stop Dewey from getting the Republican nomination. At 2 o'clock this morning Mankiewicz came running over in triumph to state that he had won the campaign for Willkie by definitely committing Harold Ross to coming out publicly for Dewey. And what PW and Mr. Winchell have done to him since beggars description.

Well, that's enough for this time. Let me know just as soon as your plans are settled for the next few weeks. And I hope to God it will be Harrisburg or some other place even nearer home.

My love to Pat, Tony and yourself.

As ever,
Bennett

P.S.   My social secretary (slang for Jezebel) reminds me that Tuesday is your wedding anniversary. My heartiest congratulations to both of you, and here's hoping it is the last one that we spend apart!

July 1, 1942

Dear Don:

All of us were staggered by the knowledge that you are practically back in the publishing business. Two months to finish one
book indeed! Why, in that time, Klopfer, Commins and I expect to turn out two volumes of Thomas Aquinas, one volume
of St. Augustine, and the Sex Life of Elmer Adler. We are torn
between pleasure at the knowledge that you are doing something you really know something about, and worry that you
will fret at such a humdrum interlude in what promised to be
the high road to adventure. Don't forget we are all pulling for
you no matter what you do, and we are still hoping that something will bring you East. Why the hell don't you tell them that
you can finish that book much faster in New York where your
former cronies will help you, if they absolutely have to.

Many thanks for the renewed invitation to use the farm. I hope
to take advantage of it either myself sometime in July, or when
Phyllis gets back in August. As I think I have written you, she is
leaving with Bubbles one week from today for the coast for a
three week vacation. Bubbles is treating her to the round trip
and both of them will be boarding with Anne Shirley, so the
price looked right to us! I urged her to go since, under present
circumstances, it is unlikely that I will get more than a week at
a time off, if that much.

Business news in a nutshell: I asked Mannie to send you the
May statement which is a pippin. June will be even better but,
of course, a lot of the profit in June will be a bit on the phony
side since we are selling thousands of dollars worth of inventory
that is marked down on our books to next to nothing. Not one
remainder was disposed of in May, however, so the May figure
is strictly kosher. The Reynolds and the Paul books keep up

beautifully. You will remember that we made a 10% free book offer on PARIS a couple of weeks ago. Yesterday Harold Williams called up and bought his third thousand on that basis! My God, how the dollars—at least the accounts receivable— roll in!

Frances Merriam is going to take Leah Daniels' place beginning Monday, and I think we are damn lucky to get her. The picture of you in uniform decided her to take the job and she has agreed to take a $10.00 cut in salary the minute you come back. My God, how you mesmerize those Macy gals.

Believe it or not, we haven't signed a contract for a new book in three weeks. Harry Maule is home today whipping the new Maritta Wolff book into shape. He says it is going to be a world beater. A new manuscript from Chris Massie arrived yesterday along with a voice from the dead in the shape of a long new novel by Morley Callighan. The Fearing novel is a complete flop, as expected. ST. LOUIS is tapering off, but will do well over 8000, which isn't bad in these times.

I honestly think that is all the news I can give you. Elliot Paul has blown into town and is waiting outside to have lunch with me. Next thing you know, you will be getting a telephone call or something from Mrs. Bennett Cerf. She should arrive on the coast about July 10th.

My love to you.

As ever,
Bennett

Aug. 11—'42

Dear Bennett—

I've neglected to write before this as I haven't known my plans. We drove across the continent in the six days allotted to us and I reported Tuesday morning.* Hoisington had arrived before me having sold a hill of goods to the training command at Ft. Worth. We've reworked the book and he's off for Ft. Worth and Washington to-morrow. If he sells the idea of printing it at an outside printer I'll be back in N.Y. next week. If not I won't be back until after the war. My present assignment is in charge of Training Aids out here. If I stay I can build up this department into something really big. We can do one helluva job but I don't know how long I'll be left here. It seems like a long way to the Harrisburg School but you never can tell what will happen in the army.

We're living at the Santa Ana Hotel until I hear from Perry next week. Saw Georgie over the week-end. He thinks he's going to get a commission in the motion picture division of the Air Corps. Which is where he belongs.

Tell Bob that I've dropped Bob Jr. [a Navy pilot] a line. . . . I'm sure I'll get him this time if he's here.

Give my love to all of the gang. . . . I left rather abruptly without telling you how grand it was to be back even for a little while. Please use the farm for your vacation. . . . And use some of my liquor. It'll spoil. Kiss Jez for me.

Love,
Donald

*Klopfer had gotten leave and returned briefly to New York.

August 31, 1942

Dear Cap:

A sudden burst of frigid weather sent us scampering home from Maine a few days ahead of schedule, and what did we do over the weekend but pack up Christopher, his nurse Margaret, his potty and various and sundry other accoutrements, took Edith and Lewis Young along as a happy afterthought, and proceed down to the Klopfer farm for as nice a weekend as I have had in a long, long time. Before I go any further, I want to thank you both very much indeed.

It rained all day Saturday and I read Maritta Wolff's NIGHT SHIFT straight through. The book could have been cut a little bit more, but it certainly has in it everything but the kitchen stove, and I think we can push it in something like the fashion that Viking adopted for THE SUN IS MY UNDOING. I have already given Johnny Beecroft a terrific sales talk on the book. Galleys are in his hands and we can only hope. While I am on the subject, Bob is handling the Dinesen negotiations with the BOMC. It is an "A" book and we are all in high hopes. The Lin Yutang looks dubious for a strange reason. Merry Wood and Harry Abrams are all for it, but Harry Scherman is very frigid about the whole scheme. The reason, believe it or not, is that he is sore as hell at Lin for his attitude on India and the Far East today. Mind you, Harry doesn't say this in so many words, but it seemed perfectly obvious to both Bob and me on separate visits. I am afraid that all those arguments that you and I had with Harry about India and so forth didn't help the situation any. It is sort of a wry joke that, after all the Chinese stuff the Club has adopted, Harry should go off on this angle just when we have something to throw into the pot! I haven't given up on the Lin book yet, but if we can jam it by Harry in his present state of mind, it will be a minor miracle.

. . .

To go on with the tale of the weekend, yesterday was perfect and we played lots of paddle tennis. The farm is in wonderful condition. The corn and the peaches are beyond description (Lewis and I each ate exactly twelve ears of corn apiece while we were there). I came in this morning on your regular train which, in honor of my presence, was forty minutes late, thus enabling me to get to the office at my usual hour and preserving Jezebel's sanity, such as it is, for another few days.

Gaston seemed really glad to see us. Marguerite* seems pretty well recovered, but now has hay fever to bother her and Gaston thinks this will retard her complete convalescence for several additional weeks. She is expecting Pat on September 9th. Is that correct? Thrup is finding out what the expenses were for the weekend and we insist on your accepting remuneration for the same. Don't forget that we agreed on this basis before you left. I don't want any shenanigans from you about it.

Business is sound and PARIS and STARS keep up amazingly. We had to borrow another twenty from the bank today to cover royalty payments, but that looks like the last trip we'll have to make to this particular well, and I honestly think that, by January 1st, we'll be financially sound, at last.

I don't quite understand your new post. If you have time, I wish you'd explain it to me a little more fully. I do hope you will be able to make New York again this Fall. I miss you badly enough at the office here, but down at the farm it gave me a strange empty feeling not to have you pottering around in your handsome blue overalls. Tell Pat I missed her very much at the farm too—honest. As for Thrup, she is your wife's devoted slave and champion.

*Gaston and Marguerite ran the Klopfer country home.

. . .

We'll take care of Sergeant Moore's manuscript when it gets here. My desk is an awful-looking mess, so I will cut this now and write again when I am caught up with myself.

Love,
Bennett

P.S. Did I tell you that I am working on an anthology of military humor for Pocket Books? I hope you will send along any funny stories connected with the war that you can think of. Keep 'em clean; this book is aimed at the army purchasing commission and the Red Cross, and if I do a decent job, I honestly think it will sell a half a million copies.

P.P.S. Just as I finished dictating this letter, Jezebel informed me that she had gotten a note from you this morning saying that the manual had been canned in Washington. Why in hell she didn't tell me this while I was dictating this note is a problem more for a psychiatrist than for myself. Does this all mean that all the months' work that has been put in on the manual goes for nothing? And is there no chance of a reversal somewhere?

Sept. 1 — 1942

Dear Bennett—

I've been a bit neglectful about writing lately but things have gotten dull around here. The Manual has been canned by Col. Smith in Washington after receiving the blessings of the Training Command in Ft. Worth. We were to do it for the whole country but I guess the Washington boys will want credit for it so they'll probably come out with one like it in time for the next war. It's pretty discouraging and is symbolic of the nonsense that still goes on here in Washington. God save me from Headquarters anywhere. I haven't gotten any details from Perry yet but I guess he'll be back in another week and then I'll hear all about his misadventures. In the meantime, we are working along here on our little projects to help out wherever we can in training these cadets so that they won't commit suicide when they have to fly against some real opposition.

We took a little house at Lido Isle—get into it September 20th—that's OK since Pat is returning to New York on Saturday and I would not want to "keep house" by myself. It has three bedrooms and two baths and is about 100 yards from the water. So if you can get out here, there's plenty of room for you. My wife will do the cooking and cleaning but it's very compact so that shouldn't be too much of a problem. I'll expect to lose weight then and I can stand it.

I seem to be further and futher from action in this job and I really miss the gang and the business like the devil. This seems like so much play when there's real work to be done.

Give my love to Thrup, Bob and the whole office. Let me hear from you once in a while.

Love,
Donald

September 4, 1942

Dear Donald:

Your letter of September 1st sounded a little down in the mouth to me, and I hope it was only a passing mood. I have got enough sense to understand your feeling of complete frustration over the manual debacle, and I also understand that the prospects of teaching a lot of squirts at Santa Ana for an indefinite period is not too glamourous. On the other hand, another shift may come along at any second and the first thing you know, you will find yourself ordered to some foreign clime. And just think, you might have been stuck down in Washington. I had dinner with Chester Kerr on Wednesday evening, and I gather that the guys who are stationed down there, both in uniform and in offices like the CWI, are in a state bordering on complete dementia. In spite of all this, things do seem to be getting done and, if the Russians can only hold in the South a little bit longer, the tide may turn once and for all.

David Ormsby's THE SOUND OF AN AMERICAN has finally been published by Dutton's and is getting incredibly mixed reviews. Some of them are devastating, but the book is going to sell, possibly better even than anything he ever did under the Longstreet handle. It certainly wasn't anything for the Random House list, even if it hits 100,000.

Yesterday's total on PARIS is exactly 846 copies, and we are well over 50,000, and I think there is another ten or fifteen thousand in the woods on it for sure. We gave Saxe a $500.00 bonus the other day for his work on the book and I am sure you will approve of this gesture. Needless to say, he was delighted.

Under separate cover, I have sent you a set of bound galleys of the Cecil Brown book. That is the next baby on which we are going to concentrate our big guns. The Maritta Wolff opus is in line to follow. You can rest easy that the Fall list is going to go over big and that everything possible is being done for it.

Frances Merriam is working out in a brilliant fashion and is a great addition to our ranks.

. . .

I wish to hell you were sitting across that desk from me at this moment.

As ever,
Bennett

P.S. I have just received the enclosed letter from Manny Piller. Will this guy be anything for us in case we found an opening? Please return his note to me along with your comments.

September 11, 1942

Dear Klopf:

At the end of a long and particularly trying day, I shall cease potching Jezebel just long enough to write you a brief report.

1. Interest in the Cecil Brown book is terrific. It's been made an "A" book along with the Dinesen [*Winter's Tales*].

Maybe out of the two, we'll get one windfall! The Philadelphia Inquirer has bought the second serial rights to SUEZ for the unbelievable sum of $1200.00 and, using this as a lever, we got the even more unbelievable sum of $1400.00 from the New York Post. Unfortunately, we had to throw the New York deal into the pot to sweeten the deal with the United Features Syndicate so, although we get half of the Philadelphia jack, we'll only get 25% of the New York sum and similar ones that follow. United Features rang up $18,000.00 worth of sales on this hitherto undreamed of end of the affair alone. We are releasing second serial rights on December 7th, which is a date that may have some connotations for you!

2. Hollywood is seemingly very excited over NIGHT SHIFT. Today, at the last moment, the William Morris office called to calmly tell us that Maritta Wolff has made them her movie agent. Harry Maule is in Maine, as you know, so Bob and I will have to try to find out what kind of idiocy this is. I told the smooth and hitherto unheard of bastard at the Morris office that his coming in at this particular time was like somebody claiming a commission for getting F.D.R. some time on the networks. I won't even give him galleys until I see what's what. We're in for 20% of these movie rights and mean to protect our interests to the last ditch, even if you have to go to jail for it!

3. Walter Black has taken RINGED WITH FIRE for his Detective Book Club.

4. We wangled Twentieth Century-Fox into buying 500 of our remaining 700 copies of THE OX-BOW INCIDENT at $1.00 a copy net.

5. Elmer Davis has written that Brown's book will go through Washington O.K. with just a few minor changes.

6. We are turning down a putrid adventure story by Randau and Zugsmith that is just a musical comedy version of THE SETTING SUN OF JAPAN. Collier's has bought it and some publisher will undoubtedly do it, but it stinks on ice and, when good old Max Lieber said we couldn't have any share of the movie rights, we gave him the old brusheroo.

7. Kenneth Fearing has turned in some stinker that he dug out of the trunk in an obvious effort to end his contract with us.

We are going to let him get away with it. I am just fed up with shenanigans of the likes of him. I hope this meets with your approval.

8. All of the above will give you a rough idea of what our business days are like right now.

Pat and Tony blew into the office to say hello on Tuesday, but we've seen no sign of her since. That evening, at about 7:30, good old Rae called up to say she was having a party for Pat and had forgotten to ask us. This squares us up for the Junior Miss party. If she ever brings that up again, I will push her teeth in. In fact, I'd be glad to do this anyhow. Thrup has been trying to get Pat over for dinner, and I hope we will be able to make a date with her when she gets her deck cleared.

Jez has promised to send you all important books from now on. Let's presume for the nonce that she knows an important book when she sees one. She'll have to prove it to me. (Faces are being made while I dictate this.)

In addition to the office work, and the Saturday Review column, I am spending countless hours at night on my Pocket Book anthology of war humor. Jesus, what a job this is turning out to be. If you know any *clean* jokes about either the Army or the Navy, for God's sake send them to me. I am particularly light on Navy stories. I think, however, that the book is going to be a reasonably amusing one—if Jez and I live long enough to finish it.

Social life is practically nil. We spent last weekend at Neysa's. This Saturday we are going down to the Guggenheims and next weekend is reserved for the Schermans, where I am going to make one more effort to put over the Lin Yutang. I still have hopes in this connection.

. . .

Well, I am back to the potching. Write soon and know that all of us here miss you terribly and love you very, very much.

As ever,
Bennett

September 17, 1942

Dear Donald:

Funny thing: Your distinctly nostalgic note about our beloved Minsk Bombshell arrived just about ten minutes after Belle Becker had come in to tell me that she had lunch today with Marion.* Incidentally, Belle reports that Marion never looked prettier or more glamorous in her life, and that she seemed happy and that Henry seems well on his way toward getting a commission somewhere or other. Speaking of anniversaries, today is my second, putting all my previous records, of course, completely to rout. Klopfer, let's face the fact that we are both rapidly approaching the A. K. stage. . . . .

Bob has wired you the BOMC news. I never really expected that they would take the Cecil Brown book and the door is still open on the Dinesen, so after the first bitter moment of disappointment, my spirits rallied pretty quickly. I agree with you that all the worst sides of Brown's personality crop up in the book and mar it to a considerable extent. We took out what we could in the editing, but you can't change a leopard's spots entirely, if I may coin a phrase. Nevertheless, I think it is going to be a wow of a best seller. The Dinesen will be reconsidered at

*Marion Anspacker Hart, Donald's first wife.

the next meeting when the judges will have a chance to read the last three stories that we are missing in the manuscript that we were able to give them for this session. Major Haas* has his heart set on consummating this deal and the Major has never let us down yet. (I'm no fool. I know he is going to see the carbon of this letter.)

Lew Miller† is in Washington, so of course Joe Margolies [a book buyer] appeared in New York today. I am going down to sell him myself tomorrow morning at 10 and hope I haven't lost the old knack of wangling good quantities from him. The only way I can describe business is to say that it is incredible. Yesterday, for instance, there were over 500 PARIS and over 250 STARS. In my next letter I am hoping to have a movie sale of NIGHT SHIFT to report to you.

Tony has approved of a lot of my jokes for the war book so I am beginning to be afraid that it stinks. And between your letters and Pat's verbal explanations, I think I am beginning to understand something about what you are doing out there. I know how you are missing the publishing business here but, on the other hand, don't forget that I am stamping around wishing to God I could get into uniform. A simple case of green pastures, my boy.

Write as often as you can.

Love,
Bennett

---

*Bob Haas stayed in the reserve after WWI and received the rank of general.
†Lewis Miller, RH sales manager.

Sept. 26, 1942

Dear Bennett—

I'm sorry I plum forgot about your anniversary. Somehow or other I thought it was nearer the end of the month. Anyway you don't have to have me tell you what I wish Thrup and you. Nothing's too good for you two and I certainly will you the moon. But I will not admit that I am getting to be an A.K. Maybe you are, but I'm just hitting the prime of life. One more month before I start to collapse!

Spent the week-end at Georgie's. He's going nuts waiting for his commission to come thru. If it doesn't I think he'll kill himself. He's about to sell his house and really sever all connections with the past. Had dinner at Kenneth McKenna's and played hearts with the boys resulting in a decided victory for the last!

I'll be curious to see about that book of yours. I haven't heard one good story of this war. And that's not kidding.

Thanks for the news about business. I hope Lew is planning to make a distribution of one juvenile as per heretofore. Charlie Howe is awaiting on it. Stopped in to see Phil Kubel on my way to Georgie's. God he looks like a corpse. I'm sure the Cecil Brown will sell like hell. How many are you printing?

No news from here. I'm flying down to San Diego tomorrow to see what the Navy has to offer. Hope I can see Bob Jr. Coming back in the late afternoon. Won't give me much time.

My love to all at the office. I miss you guys like hell! Potch Jez for me. Is Saxe O.K. or killing himself with work. Watch out for him.

Love,
Donald

September 29, 1942

Dear Don:

Since you are busy defending Democracy, it fell to the lot of Maestro Luigi Miller and myself to journey up to Boston on Thursday for a party thrown by the Hillyers in honor of MY HEART FOR HOSTAGE. The party was staged at the new Hillyer home at 39 Pinckney Street. Dorothy has done a wonderful job of decorating the place; it looks like a miniature edition of Hampshire House. And boy, did she draw out the crowd for this party. Alfred McIntyre, Henry Houghton (proxy at Houghton Mifflin), the Ray Everitts, the John Dos Passos', the Benny de Votos, Ted Weeks, Bush Campbell, Dick Fuller, Alice Bond, Mark Schorer and God knows who else turned up—over 90 guests in all, with a buffet supper, champagne, and an accordion player to enliven the proceedings. The party began at 5 and ended at 2 in the morning, and I should say it was a huge success. . . . Dale Warren and Mrs. Dos Passos executed a rhumba so gracefully that they fell down a flight of stairs. George Frazier brought his new wife, Mimsie, who is an absolute knockout. I thought it was good policy to devote a little of my own time to one of our author's wives. . . . Alice Bond ended her feud with Dorothy Hillyer long enough to pose for a picture with Dorothy and Dick Fuller. Only a few people vomited. What with one thing and another, the party certainly reminded me of our famous shindig at Princeton two years ago.

Incidentally, Bush Campbell, while he was still coherent, said some wonderful things about you and, in fact, everybody in Boston has been so taken in by that superficial charm of yours that not one of them realizes what a terrible bastard you really are underneath.

. . .

Business news is scarce at the moment, but our big books are now in the offing and the dam will soon bust. We had lunch with Quent Reynolds yesterday. He is going to dash off a quickie for us on the Dieppe affair which will probably be called "Dress Rehearsal." Selwyn James has turned in his manuscript of SOUTH OF THE CONGO. With a little fixing, it will be an important book about the one part of the world that hasn't been covered yet, and I think it will be good for 6000 at least. Another piece of the Sheean manuscript has come in just about on scheduled time. Red Lewis, as I told you, promised us his complete manuscript for Christmas day. The movie rights to NIGHT SHIFT have not yet been sold, but I think Warners will sign up at any minute. Ben Zevin just sent in contracts for reprint editions of THE MAN WITH NO FACE, WATCH ON THE RHINE, and VOLTAIRE'S PHILOSOPHICAL DICTIONARY—the last one of Luigi's Carlton House numbers. (Remember?) There is nothing to stop PARIS and STARS. Even HAYS NONNY NONNY may surprise us. Harry Bull just called up and bought one of the chapters for TOWN AND COUNTRY for 300 bucks.

I am now getting all my advance material together on the Lin Yutang for one more onslaught on the Harry Scherman citadel. The news on the other new books can wait for another time, but baby, it's all good. It looks like Jezebel will be wearing sables before the war is over—that is, if she is willing to comply with certain conditions that I have set forth.

I have been slaving night after night on that damn war humor anthology and hope to turn the finished manuscript in to Bob de Graff sometime next week. If anybody so much as breathes a war joke to me after that period, I will probably club him with a baseball bat.

I was sorry to hear about Pat's illness. I am sure everything will be okay in a couple of days.

We miss you more all the time.

As ever,
Bennett

Oct. 1, 1942

Dear Bennett,

Thanks for taking Patsy out in New York. The kid has had a busy time between her family, my family and closing up the farm. She writes me that you're crammed full of the joke book. I haven't heard a decent clean story about this war. I hope there are some around, but they don't percolate thru' to this rare atmosphere.

This week I went up to Victorville for a day. It's a bombardier school and advanced flying. I flew for about 2½ hours in the bombardier's seat in the nose of the ship. You are surrounded by nothing but transparent plastic and believe me you get a wonderful view of everything. We flew over Lake Arrowhead and the mountains and into Arizona. Came back and a friend of mine flew me back to Santa Ana, letting me take the controls for a while. I think I'd make a hot pilot. If I'm ever transferred to a small field I'm going to learn to fly. It's the only way to get around this part of the world with a 35 mi. speed limit.

Business goes on as usual. I hope R.H. does too. Mannie writes we may be able to pay off the 20M to-day and the balance the end of the month. That would be great. I'm keeping fingers crossed for Blyer. Will you tell Jez I have not received a single book from R.H. out here! Only Brown proofs.

My love to the gang. I miss all of you. Kiss Thrup for me and tell her she ought to write me a long love letter.

Love,
Donald

October 6, 1942

Dear Don:

I was bowled over by your two letters which arrived here simultaneously yesterday. The thought of you actually flying a plane has me so green with envy that one of our new nearsighted employees on the eighth floor mistook me for an advance copy of Peter Rainier's GREEN FIRE.

The intelligence test certainly sounds as though something might be stirring, and I am sure I don't have to tell you I hope you get what you want. Personally, I wish they'd transfer you to some post within twenty miles of here, so we can see that granite-like puss of yours once in a while. I was terribly sorry to hear about Georgie's commission falling through. What the hell happened?

. . .

Here's the last-minute news from Random House in a nutshell. Warner's bought NIGHT SHIFT today for $25,000.00. We are in for 20%, which is only terrific, if you get what I mean. SUEZ TO SINGAPORE has been raised to $3.50, and I am sure you will agree with the wisdom of this move when you see how imposing the book actually looks. We are printing 40,000 copies of this little baby, and I don't see what can stop it. Second serial rights have already been sold to New York, Philadelphia, Boston, Detroit, Akron and Miami, and Colin Miller is out now on a special trip for United Features to work on this book alone. I honestly believe that our share on second serial rights alone will top $3000.00 by the time we are finished.

Selwyn James has delivered the manuscript of his South African book. It is going to be called SOUTH OF THE CONGO and, after a little fixing up by the old maestro Commins, should be a strong entry for our Spring list.

That old stinker Watt cabled that Graves refused to make any changes in his novel on the life of Milton and offered to let us out of the contract if we felt so inclined. We felt so inclined; in fact, we broke a couple of legs getting the cable off to tell him so. That is a palooka off our hands and no mistake.

The rest of our business is simply incredible. The Monday invoices are on my desk and the pile is so high it will take me three trips to the can to get through them. I have promised De Graff the complete manuscript for the War Book a week from today, so that headache will soon be off my mind. My social life has been nil except for the ball game on Saturday and yesterday. Satenstein was the host yesterday, and Milo Sutliff and Frank Henry were the other members of the party. The poor old Yanks never had a prayer; the Cards simply rushed them off their feet. I would say something about tempus fugit, but what's the use of talking Latin to a dumb bastard like you.

Love,
Bennett

October 16, 1942

CAPTAIN DONALD S. KLOPFER

DINESEN A DUAL SELECTION. AS I ALWAYS SAID IT'S A WONDERFUL BOARD OF JUDGES. LOVE AND KISSES

BENNETT

Oct. 16, 1942

Dear Benito—

Thanks a thousand fold for the telegram announcing the good news of La Belle Dinesen. It's really very exciting and our good partner RKH [Random House Knopf Warehouse] must be in a disgusting state of self satisfaction. I always did like the Danes, but what's happened to the Chinese. Old Lin Yu Tang has lost the golden touch I take it because he doesn't think the British are God's gift to this war. I think we'll do damned well with the book anyway, but it would make such a good dividend!

Pat got back last Sunday, felt rotten on Monday, had the doctor down on Tuesday and on Tuesday night was in the Cedars of Lebanon Hospital in Hollywood. She came out too soon after her operation and was completely pooped so she had to go somewhere where she would be taken care of, namely in hospital. I've been driving up there each night so I haven't had much chance to write. I hope she'll be out to-morrow or Sunday and will go over to Edgar's for a few days. She can't come back here until she's really strong as she has to do all of her own work. Servants just are impossible to find out here. Incidentally, Cerfie, Pat says that the date she had with you was one of the two dates she had other than family while in N.Y. Thanks for taking her out.

My department is clicking along in all four these days. We're badly stuck for lack of space but that can't be helped until they give us a building of our own. That will come along soon and then we can be well organized. I've really been working hard lately, believe it or not!

My best love to everyone around the place. I miss all of you like the devil. Potch Thrup for me—

All love,
Donald

October 19, 1942

Dear Bennett:

Thanks for your letter of October 16th with the figures attached thereto. It looks to me as though we were romping ahead at a pretty good pace. I am glad to see that SPY NOV-

ELS is over the 5,000 mark and I am sure it will continue to sell. PAN-AMERICAN SPANISH also looks as though it would go on for a long time. In fact, I can't see anything to complain about as far as business is concerned. According to Pauline's figures, October should be a "wow" of a month. I hope to God that Harry Sherman really gets a fond reaction to his test mailing on the LIN YUTANG. It is really wonderful news about the Dinesen book. I passed Marian Hunter's book shop yesterday (Sunday) and she had a fine display of SUEZ TO SINGAPORE in the window—one week before publication date. That's what I like to see in a book seller.

Pat is out of the hospital now but staying up at Beverly for the balance of this week. After that, I feel sure that she will be well enough to come down and cook for me. Laugh that off. With regard to your insulting remarks about Pauline—to me she looks like a combination of Hedy Lamarr, Greta Garbo, and Ann Sheridan. I'll bet she is just as glad to get rid of that damn joke book as you are. I saw Private Oppenheimer yesterday and he is happy as a lark in his new guise of a buck private. The rear view of him in G.I. OD's looks a little bit like Oliver Hardy wandering down Wilshire Boulevard. I am delighted to hear that you have gotten mixed up in the Council on Books in war Time. I doubt if you can fill my shoes but at least you can try,

As always,
Donald

October 30, 1942

Dear Don:

How come these beautifully typewritten letters? Have you managed to snag some beautiful young WAAC to act as your secretary? And if you are, is she as potchable as Jezebel? This letter is being typed by an absolute stranger since Jezebel went into a swoon when she read your remark that she looked like a combination of Lamarr, Garbo and Sheridan, and we have not been able to revive her since. The poor creature has become more gullible than your first bride. (Remember?)

I take it that you have received your detailed copy of the September statement. The profit figure simply staggered me. Klopfer, my boy, you are getting rich while you sit on that fat can of yours idling away the time in sunny California. At least, you are getting rich on paper. At least you are getting rich until the Government takes it all away from you, which will be any minute now. Seriously, we are going to have one hell of a tax problem this year unless I can mark the Greek Drama and the Duplaix swag to minus 10¢ a copy instead of plus. I have a conference on tap with Senor Podoll to see if we can institute some kind of a dividend system or something, which will make the rap as painless as possible. We are out of the bank, at last, and unless some utterly unforeseen catastrophe occurs, there really ought to be some cash rolling around here in short order.

We gave Ann Rann a raise from $40.00 to $60.00, and Frances Merriam an equal $10.00 boost. We also gave Florence a $4.00 raise. These three girls have been doing wonderful work for us. I am particularly delighted with Frances Merriam. I am enclosing herewith a direct mailing piece which she worked out for the Modern Library, and also a throw away for the Lin Yutang. I hope you will agree that they are absolutely top notch.

. . .

She has certainly been a great addition to the Random House ranks. The kids on the eighth floor are slaving religiously and, when Christmas time comes around, we expect, with your permission, to hand out some really substantial bonuses. I suppose we'll have to give some good raises too, to everybody, that is, but Jezebel, who is willing to take it out in love. Anyhow, she obviously has an outside income because she certainly didn't get those two mink coats and that sable wrap on the salary she makes here.

SUEZ TO SINGAPORE looks like an absolute smash. The News Company reordered 1000 yesterday, and Marshall Field reordered 250. The next two weeks should tell us just how big it is going to be. Hillyer's MY HEART FOR HOSTAGE and Samuel Adams' THE HARVEY GIRLS are both pleasant surprises, and we'll make plenty on both of them. The complete Sheean is in and we also have the first draft of Sinclair Lewis' book, so both of these are sure for February.

My desk is piled so high that it has flowed over onto yours, and I am going slightly bats. Forgive me if this letter is a little bit incoherent. God damn it, how I wish you were here with us!

As ever,
Bennett

November 3, 1942

Dear Bennett:

The secret of those beautifully typewritten letters is that I inherited a secretary from the good old Hoisington days and I can't get rid of her. The only trouble with her is that there are approximately 15,000 so called cadets on the field ranging in age from 20 to 26 and she is constantly going around and getting herself engaged to one or another of these flea-bitten youngsters. It is perfectly obvious that she doesn't appreciate the wisdom and beauty of maturity, besides which, she is constantly pining for Hoisington. So you may know that all my loyalty and love are for my beautiful Pauline, who should constantly be swooning over me unless she is silly enough to fall for your fumbling potching.

Yes, I was terribly pleased to get the financial statement and now that my Uncle Sam is protecting me by forbidding you thieves from raising your salaries, maybe we'll get luscious dividends out of Random House. But all kidding aside, you know I heartily approve of giving substantial bonuses for the whole office if we have the dough in the bank; but don't forget Miller's 2% on volume over $50,000. He's going to get a big wad again this year. Keep those in your calculations. Obviously Pauline doesn't need a raise. If she has only two fur coats, she is holding out on you. I gave her three myself—sable, chinchilla, and ermine.

I am delighted to continue to get news of good business. I hope SUEZ TO SINGAPORE hits 100,000. All my work here continues to pile in on me so that I am deluged. I can't see when I will ever get away from this God damn post.

Give my love to everyone at the office.

As always,
Donald

P.S.   You forgot to enclose the mailing piece for Modern Library and LIN YUTANG. I wish to Hell I were back with you!

Nov. 7, 1942

Dear Bennett,

I received the copy of Dinesen yesterday and read some of the stories last night. The gal really is one hell of a good writer. And boy, did our Robert K. spend dough on that book to bring the price up to 2.75. Two-color half titles, title page and sheets and a two cloth binding. I'll bet that's the last bit of real old-fashioned extravagance until after the war. It's really an impressive job and don't ever let the Colonel razz you about blurbs again. He must have really liked that book! I've heard vague rumours that our October volume was the biggest ever. Here's hoping they don't come bouncing back on us! Does Suez to Singapore really look like a smash?

I've been working all over again revising the manual once more. They tell me the way has been paved to have it published in Washington at the GPO and I've had to do some more work on it. I should finish that by the end of next week and then it'll probably be rejected again! That, plus all of my normal work makes my time pretty well occupied but I can't complain. I seem to be getting to be the general utility man around this field, which is fun but is a helluva way to win a war. I hope to hell that the British are really pushing the Germans around in Africa. It looks kosher but I don't trust the news reports.

My spies tell me that you've been working like a beaver. Has Bob's new job meant very much more time for him to be away from the office—or is it mostly night work? Remember the old ML days when neither of us did a damned thing and we really made some money?

Pat's back on the job again and feeling okay for a change. I hope she stays that way.

Give my best to all the office people. I sure do miss all of you and wish I were back again bothering around with all the details of the publishing business which are really so much fun. My love to Thrup and Chris—

Love,
Donald

November 9, 1942

Dear Don:

I don't suppose you see my column in the Saturday Review any more, thereby missing one of the great literary treats of the day—so I am enclosing herewith a copy of a recent column in which I credited you with a pretty funny gag. No charge for this service.

I am also enclosing a copy of a whopping ad that we ran in the past few days in both the Times and the Tribune and will repeat in a few other papers scattered about the country. I figure that we might as well make a big splurge in advertising in the next couple of months; Mr. Morgenthau will be paying most of the bills.

Your comment about my fumbling potching has stirred me into fresh efforts, so I have no more time to dictate letters to the likes of you. Upward and onward is my motto. Incidentally, I wish to hell you'd stick to your own territory.

Resentfully,
Bennett

Bennett conceived of an anthology of inspirational writings to be edited by Lloyd C. Douglas, author of the international best-seller The Robe, *and turned to Donald for help since Douglas lived in California. The situation was further complicated by the fact that Douglas was published by Houghton Mifflin.*

November 9, 1942

CAPTAIN DONALD S. KLOPFER

THINK IT POSSIBLE THAT YOU CAN DO A GREAT TURN FOR RANDOM HOUSE OVER WEEKEND. CAN YOU PHONE ME SOMETIME TONIGHT. DON'T CARE WHAT HOUR YOU WAKE ME. I WILL BE HOME ALL EVENING. CRAZY TO TALK TO YOU ANYHOW.

BENNETT

November 10, 1942

Dear Donald:

Between my phone conversation with you last night and the Colonel's letter (under my tutelage you will notice that his literary style is showing signs of improvement) I think you've got about all the ammunition we can give you for your onslaught on Lloyd Douglas. I can only add the following:

1. The 300 to 350 page length is the merest suggestion. If Douglas thinks it ought to go to another 100 pages more or so, that, of course, is up to him.

2. Be sure that you stress the spiritual side of the project as much as the financial one. If we can sell Douglas the idea that he will be making a terrific contribution to American morale and that the Office of War Information is very, very keen about the notion (which indeed is the truth) he may undertake the project as a patriotic duty. That doesn't mean, of course, that you won't impress upon him the fact that if this thing sells the way it ought to, he'll make a lot of money out of it. Furthermore, it should continue selling for years, which will mean royalties for him when he is old and gray. (I may burst into tears at any moment.)

3. Linscott's exact words to me were: "The question of Lloyd Douglas is a toughie. Greater love hath no publisher than to release his most profitable author to a rival house. Nevertheless, I don't see why you shouldn't feel free to proposition him. If he is attracted to your suggestion and asks our advice, we shall feel free, at that time, to advise him either for or against it depending upon his plans and his desires." I want to be absolutely sure that Douglas realizes that we had permission of Houghton Mifflin before approaching him at all.

4. Please tell Douglas that Bob Linscott at Houghton Mifflin is anxious to see the table of contents and may make a few valuable suggestions to us.

5. Assure Douglas that the book will be advertised very widely, but also in an extremely dignified manner. It will undoubt-

edly get tremendous attention from the critics who may not have rated his novels as the finest kind of literature. You will have to put this point over delicately, but I am sure you know what I mean. I have a hunch that Douglas, in his heart, yearns for the plaudits from guys like Fadiman and Gannett, as well as big sales to the low-brows.

6. If possible, we'd like to get a completed manuscript some-time along about March so that we can bring the book out in late summer or early fall, with plenty of advance build-up and promotion.

Good luck, toots, and if any other points come up while you're with Douglas, I take it for granted that you will either call up long distance while you are actually with him, or get in touch with us immediately thereafter. We are counting on you to bring home the bacon.

I can't tell you how delighted I was to hear your voice over the phone. We ought to do this oftener—once every three weeks at least.

As ever,
Bennett

1942 NOV 13 AM 2 10
BENNETT A CERF=RANDOM HOUSE

RECEIVED ALL YOUR DOPE SHEETS THANKS HAVE
WRITTEN DOUGLAS FOR APPOINTMENT SUNDAY
AS HIS TELEPHONE IS UNLISTED WISH ME LUCK
LOVE=

DONALD.

1942 NOV 16 AM 8 48
BENNETT A CERF=

DOUGLAS REFUSES TO DO BOOK BUT SUGGEST
EITHER FOSDICK OR HALFORD LUCCOCK YALES
SCHOOL OF RELIGION SORRY I FUMBLED THE BALL
LETTER FOLLOWS LOVE=

DONALD.

November 16, 1942

CAPTAIN DONALD S. KLOPFER

WOULD IT INTEREST YOU TO KNOW THAT WE
HAVE JUST GOTTEN ANOTHER BOOK OF THE

MONTH CLUB DUAL SELECTION. IT IS GUADAL-
CANAL DIARY AND IF YOU WILL PHONE ME AFTER
ONE OCLOCK TONIGHT EASTERN TIME I WILL
GIVE YOU THE GLORIOUS DETAILS. LOVE.

BENNETT

November 21, 1942

Dear Bennett:

I am enclosing herewith a short manuscript from Charlie
Lederer, written by his wife, Virginia, who can't spell and can't
write. None the less, since several of your friends appear in this
manuscript, I thought you would be interested in reading it.

I have been pledged to secrecy about the manuscript and
have pledged you to the same secrecy, since it is a pretty mali-
cious bit.

I still think the funniest thing about it is the spelling.

As always,
Donald

November 27, 1942

Dear Don:

I am returning under separate cover Virginia Lederer's manuscript, along with Charlie's letter concerning same. The script
arrived Wednesday night and Phyllis and I read it with consid-

erable glee yesterday. The spelling, as you say, is atrocious, but I don't think the story is nearly as bad as you seem to believe. The characterizations, as a matter of fact, are really excellent, and her summary of Mildred and Eddie Knopf is nothing short of brilliant. Of course, there is not enough for a book in the script, but it seems to me that if the story were tightened a little bit, she would have no trouble at all selling it to a magazine. The one phony touch in the story is the scene at the police court. That should be completely rewritten. The other stuff, with the names changed, of course, is right good! Mum will be the word around here on this manuscript. You can assure the lady of that!

I saw Pat yesterday and she sounded quite hopeful about your getting to Washington. I sure hope you make it, toots.

As ever,
Bennett

December 15, 1942

Dear Don:

Over the weekend I read the most exciting manuscript that I have ever come across in my life. It is the full story from beginning to end of the Tokyo raid as told by Captain Ted Lawson to Bob Considine. Ted is the boy who lost a leg in the raid and who appeared with me on the Council show last Sunday night. The book is done with complete simplicity and dignity and when I didn't have tears in my eyes, I was so excited by the story that beads of perspiration stood out on my forehead.

Today Saxe, Belle* and Aaron† have locked themselves into their office and are reading the book now. They are just as completely undone by it as I was.

The big catch, of course, will be getting the book through censorship in Washington. I don't know what the odds are on this. Of course, the whole story would have to be released to the public first, but that would only add to the excitement of the book. I have got a deal all lined up with Considine and Lawson depending on Washington's okay. We'll probably sign a tentative contract tomorrow. They mentioned an advance of $5000.00, and I voluntarily raised that to $7500.00, probably establishing a precedent in the publishing business. I can only say that if this book goes through, I will bet even money that it sells a minimum of 100,000 copies. I will also bet even money that it is a Book-of-the-Month Club choice. It makes our GUADALCANAL DIARY sound like Irving Fineman's JACOB. If I possibly can, I will smuggle the manuscript out to you by the end of the week with the understanding that you won't tell a soul about it and will mail it back to me the moment you've finished it. Even if we don't get the book, the reading of it will give you the most exciting two hours that I think you have ever had in your life. (I have not gone crazy. What I am telling you here is my sincere and true feeling.) I have invited Lawson and his wife and little baby to come up and spend Christmas with us. I hope he will be able to make it. He is at the Walter Reed Hospital, but I think he can get off for a few days. After you've read the story, you will understand why I asked him for Christmas!

I haven't told you much about Phyllis and Christopher. Chris walks by himself now and is making a mighty effort to talk. He

*Belle Becker, RH editor.
†Aaron Sussman, RH advertising account.

is really a cute brat and I am crazy about him. Phyllis spends her mornings learning stenography and her afternoons with Peggy Goldman at the USO. She is doing a fine job there and I have heard about her work from several outside sources. I am really proud of her.

I have got my fingers crossed that you will be in New York for at least a few days sometime within the next month. I can't tell you how much I miss you.

As ever,
Bennett

1943

Dear Don:

It looks like Ray Freiman is all signed, sealed and delivered for the manufacturing job at Random House. He had been working for Haddon and Mel Friedman has given him as glowing a recommendation as I have ever heard in my life. He was first suggested to us by Harry Abrams, who says he is the answer to all our prayers. Bob will undoubtedly be writing you further details about this. I will keep you posted on how the thing works out.

No soap on the Sheean book for the BOMC. They selected, at yesterday's meeting, some book on the American Revolution published by an obscure little firm that needs the dough. I think their name is Little Brown. They also selected some Russian book published by Scribner's. They have now got more reserves than the U.S. Treasury.

I have been devoting the week to entertaining stray Random House authors and at the moment am so fed up that I'd be willing to swap jobs temporarily with any fairly second-rate pants presser. Sunday we were with Budd Schulberg. He is an unhappy fellow and his marriage seems wrecked beyond repair. . . . Monday night we took Red Lewis and Marcella to Jessel's show, and then picked up Jessel and repaired to the Stork Club. Jessel's certainly getting a kick out of the book he is writing for us. He took a half page ad in last week's Variety to advertise it. We've always been looking for an author who would advertise his own books, but now that we've found him, I am not exactly sure I know what to do with him.

Tuesday night we went to dinner at Quent's with Moss Hart, George Kaufman, and Mark Hanna. Mark's got a new gal named Mrs. Emmett who is an absolute knockout. Quent may be off any moment for Russia, China and India. The boys are crazy about DRESS REHEARSAL and, between ourselves, I wouldn't be surprised if it ended up by outselling the Sheean opus. Now that the BOMC has turned down the Sheean, we might as well face the fact that we are probably going to take a first-class shellacking on it. What the hell; Morgenthau should worry.

Kaufman told us about meeting a man who is going around town with a saw cutting all the wooden toilet seats in half. He explained that he expected some half-assed relatives in town.

Business continues to be excellent. SUEZ goes sailing along (another 1000 from the News yesterday) and the Lin Yutang is really catching on all over the country. The only new book that has been signed up since you left is a long novel called RETREAT FROM ROSTOV by an unknown writer. I don't know whether anyone has written to you about this as yet. I haven't read the script myself, but Saxe and a couple of the salesmen are ecstatic about it.

I hope you will have to come East again with the Manual.

My deep love,

As ever,
Bennett

January 19, 1943

Dear Klopfer:

Word has reached me from an unusually unreliable source (Jezebel, of course) that January 23rd is your natal day. This is just a line to tell you that I think of you every time Jezebel reminds me, and to assure you that I would much rather have you sitting at your desk across from me than the schlemiel who is at present desecrating your throne.

Seriously, Don, here's hoping that this is the last birthday you spend away from all of us at Random House.

My love,
Bennett

January 22, 1943

Dear Don:

I am terribly sorry to hear that the Manual seems to be footch. (Speaking of which, did you know that Jezebel once made a bowl of footch? Needless to say, it stank.) Does all this mean that the infinite amount of work that went into the Manual has been wasted, or is there still a Chinaman's chance that the project may be revived?

By this time you have no doubt studied the November report. In my opinion it is almost incredible. If this were only 1911, before income taxes went into effect, I'd point out to you that you would now be a rich young man, Captain Klopfer. As it is, I wouldn't give you credit for a damaged copy of the Public Papers of Woodrow Wilson.

I am sure Bob has told you about the 10% cut in paper. This isn't very serious, but the Council feels that this is only a starter, and that the pinch will really hit us in three or four months. Well, cancer shmancer, as long as Jezebel still has her fanny.

Write soon.

Love and kisses,
Bennett

January 29, 1943

Dear Klopf:

Under my careful guidance you are turning into something of a humorist. There were roars of laughter throughout the establishment when we heard of your new occupation. It will add to your pleasure to know that you spoiled my lunch hour. I have been trying in vain to figure out some way I can use your story in Trade Winds, but this time I am afraid I will have to give up. To get even with you, I am enclosing a picture of the Immortal Sergeant. Add this to any part of the inventory you see fit.

. . .

We are still dithering around with the Tokyo manuscript. All kinds of pressure is being brought to bear in Washington, not only from Collier's and ourselves, but from the O.W.I., which seems to be solidly on our side. Between ourselves, the whole O.W.I. seems to have about as much to say in Washington as the aforementioned Oppenbopper once did at Viking. Some day Elmer Davis is going to throw that job in some fuehrer's face!

Business continues to be fantastic. Yesterday's total included over 1600 GUADALCANAL, over 700 CHINA, and over 500 SUEZ. The specter that hangs over our heads is paper rationing. Malcolm Johnson swears that there will be a 40% cut before the year is over. Even discounting that by 50%, you can see that we'll be in a hell of a jam. I spent yesterday up in Pleasantville at the Reader's Digest plant, and maybe you think they are not worried. Their circulation jumped a cool three million last year to the unbelievable total of 9,200,000. They don't know what the hell to do now.

Speaking of post exchanges, Paul Sampliner is now a Captain and his job will be travelling around from one exchange to another checking on stock and all that sort of thing. I wouldn't wish a job like that on John Macrae Jr!

Have you ever thought of going to Africa instead of Peyrouten? If not, for Christ sake stop diddling around there in California and come back to Random House. We need you like all get out.

Love to you and Pat,
Bennett

. . .

P.S. We are taking Herbert Wise and Nell Farnol to the opening of the Kingsley play tonight. It should be quite an evening, what with one thing and another!

February 1, 1943

Dear Bennett:

I just got back from spending Sunday up at Edgar Selwyn's, and found out to my surprise that Metro had the manuscript of Thirty Seconds over Tokyo and had made synopses for all of their producers, as is their wont. Since I know you had some copies struck off for the BOMC and then decided it would be stupid to circulate it widely, and I think that is a very wise decision, I'd still like a copy to show to the C.O. out here. It would be stamped Confidential and will be treated as an Army confidential document. As such, we cannot possibly get into trouble because, after all, that's exactly how all of the intelligence reports of a similar nature are classified.

I only hope that we are not getting the run-around on this manuscript. I take it that King Features must have sent it out to Metro and probably to all the other studios. Now that his NIBS is back in Washington, maybe you will be able to take some action on this book. All of the details are gradually coming out. It doesn't make sense for them not to allow it to be published.

Pat got here last Wednesday and is returning to New York on Friday. She looks and acts fine, but I think it makes sense for her to go back and get a final clean-up before she comes out here permanently.

The November figures are really fantastic. I am very curious to see the December ones. What was our volume in January, and how is Guadalcanal Diary selling? Any chance of getting a set of proofs on the Red Lewis book?

We continue to wade around in a sea of mud but manage to keep busy. The war news certainly looks good, but I still think that our bet is a cinch for me. I miss all of you big business executives like the very devil. Give my love to the office.

As always,
Donald

February 18, 1943

Dear Don:

I have been hoping that you would call me one of these nights so I could explain the TOKYO business to you in detail.

Meanwhile, let me explain that I have given my word of honor to Col. Fitzgerald in General Searles' office in Washington that not a copy of the manuscript will leave the Random House safe. They were sore as hell when they heard that we had let the judges of the Book of the Month Club read this script, and this was the only way I could make my peace with them. I am sure I don't have to explain to you that there was a darn good reason why I didn't send a copy of the manuscript out to you.

. . .

GUADALCANAL is almost up to 40,000 and Quent Reynolds'
book looks like another runaway.

And if I don't get away soon I will probably bite somebody's
head off (probably Jezebel's).

Please call us as soon as you are able to.

As ever,
Bennett

May 11, 1943
Dear Don:

I got the first word of your transfer to Idaho on Monday morning in one of Jezebel's characteristically unintelligible commu-
niques. I immediately called New York in the hope of talking to
you before you left, and found that you were already on your
way. I am sorry I missed you but, judging by your letters to me
and Bob, you are just about set for what you've been dreaming
about, and if you don't think I envy you from the bottom of my
heart, you're nuts.

Thrup and I got just what we wanted in Florida. We were lo-
cated in a little dump about two blocks north of that monstrous
old Hollywood Beach Hotel, now populated by about 10,000
sailors. We spent practically the entire day lying on the beach

and along toward the end of our stay, I played a little ninth rate tennis with the local minister, who was just about good enough to keep me moving around the court, and who tst tsted every time I yelled "God damn." I really feel fine now and I am darn glad I went.

There is nothing new to report around the office except the trifling matter of an order for juvenile flats from Woolworth's that totals about $300,000. We are going into a huddle with Duplaix tomorrow about where in heck the books are going to come from. Then we'll frame the order and hang it alongside that Macy Modern Library document in the can.

Galleys have already been sent to you on the Tokyo book. Despite the fact that there has been so much about the raid in Life and all the newspapers, I still think that this book may blow the roof off and make a new top for Random House. With all the best sellers we have had this year we still haven't hit that magic $100,000 mark, which we simply must get to if Jezebel is to wear the clothes that she thinks she is entitled to.

Red Lewis was at the house last night on the eve of his departure for Minnesota. Harry [Scherman of BOMC] and Bernadine came over too. They scarcely knew Red, but it was a case of love at first sight when one of Red's impersonations made Harry actually cry with laughter. Lewis was ready to marry him on the spot. We couldn't get them out of the house. Tonight we are having Peg Byrnes for dinner. (George is off in Texas somewhere.) That's about the extent of our social life for the week. Saturday we are going to Alicia's, where we'll probably get into another fight [with Captain Patterson] about the God damn Daily News.

. . .

My love to Pat. Please write all details of your new assignment.
I needn't tell you how deeply interested I am in knowing exactly what you are up to.

My love,
Bennett

May 14, 1943

CAPTAIN DONALD KLOPFER
382nd BOMBARDMENT GROUP
POCATELLO, IDAHO

BOOK CLUB JUST CHOSE TOKYO AS PART OF DUAL
SELECTION FOR AUGUST. LOVE.
          BENNETT

May 17, 1943

Dear Don:

Thanks for your note about your reason for not phoning me. I
wasn't exactly hurt, since I realized that you were probably running around like a chicken without a head. Put it rather that I

was disappointed that I didn't speak to you before you left for Idaho—and then forget it.

You can imagine how delighted all of us were to have Tokyo picked by the Book Club. It goes out as a dual with something called THE ORIGIN OF THE AMERICAN REVOLUTION, which doesn't sound too hot to me but, on the other hand, WINTER'S TALES goes out with COMBINED OPERA-TIONS, so the luck sort of evens up. I must reluctantly admit that Colonel Haas did one hell of a job in retrieving Tokyo after it was practically turned down for good at the last meeting. Coming on top of his efforts in behalf of WINTER'S TALES, it seems to me that the exploit called for official recognition and, with your permission, I am putting a gold star on his report card next month. Wire if you have any objections to this.

Your telegram announcing that it snowed yesterday is startling. How much flying are you actually doing yourself? And is it as much fun as you anticipated? Give with the details, Klopfer!

We had a wonderful weekend down at Alicia's with only one fight over the Patterson family. George Abbott was there, and so was George Backer, the latter just back from the Refugee Conference in Bermuda. I gathered from his guarded remarks that it was mostly talk down there, and that nothing very constructive was done for the poor old Yids. The highlight of the day came when Mrs. Bennett A. Cerf hung up a score of 189 at the bowling alley. She had six strikes—four of them in a row—and was so excited she couldn't talk for an hour. Her name will go up on the wall as the lady champion of Falais. Harry is being given command of a field of his own at Trenton and moves down there about June 1st.

· · ·

That's about all at the moment. I am enclosing herewith Collier's ad that ran on the first installment of Tokyo.

My love to you and Pat.

As ever,
Bennett

May 22, 1943

Dear Bennett—

Thanks for your note. I'm sure that Bob did a real job with the BOMC on the Tokyo book and I'm sure we'll sell a helluva lot of them. By the way, I see the Jessel book is out! How about sending me a copy?

As far as flying is concerned I can fly as much as I please but I refuse to fly with anything less than a pilot instructor. These crazy kids don't know what the hell it's all about and when they start to take up 18 tons and 4000 h.p. it aint safe! That's a lot of airplane to crash up and I have very little desire to bail out! As soon as my work becomes better regimented I intend to fly a few missions, but I promise you I'll be in the lead ship with an experienced pilot. We've lost three ships since I've been here and it's not the fault of the B24! I'm waiting for the big boss to come thru' any day now and find out what the score really is. I'll probably have to go down to Orlando to a month of school before I'm assigned to the outfit with which I'll go overseas. I must admit that I am so sick of training outfits that I shudder at the thought of more months of it—but the whole thing makes sense. I guess the trouble is that Combat Intelligence officers don't get killed quickly enough!

This letter should get to you on your birthday. Congratulations and best wishes on your 45th. I wish I could be with you to celebrate—but we never seem to get together on your birthday. Be good. My love to Thrup and the gang.

As always
Donald

Note: During World War II there was a serious shortage of paper.

May 28, 1943

Dear Don:

This is just to tell you that we fixed up an agreement yesterday designed to net us additional paper for between 400,000 and 500,000 flats [juvenile books]. It was worked with a guy named J.A. Richards, president of J.A. Richards, Inc., publishers, Minneapolis. We have made a contract with him whereby he will be the publisher of said flats, Whitman will be the manufacturing agents, and we will be distributors. There is 110 tons of paper involved and the fee we are paying Richards for "supervision" is $13,200.00, or at the rate of 8¢ for every pound of paper used.

The next step will be a contract between Whitman and ourselves, the basis of which will be that Whitman will credit us as books are produced with 3¢ for each pound of paper used until one-half the $13,200.00 has been reached. Some of these books will presumably have to be manufactured outside Whitman's regular string of plants and such books would cost more than they normally would. We in turn will agree to split that extra cost with Whitman. If, of course, it would seem that certain books will cost more than either of us could afford, then we just won't make those. It is a complicated deal all around but, according to our two lawyers, will stand the complete scrutiny of the WPB, and I have just tried to give you the highlights.

Smith and Durrell are apparently on the rocks, and we are looking into the possibility of taking them over. They have assets including a written-down inventory of about $23,000.00, and liabilities, mostly accounts payable, of about the same. They want $28,000.00 for the business, they to assume the liabilities. The potential advantages, from our point of view, are, in the first place, that they have lost $24,000.00 during the last two years and, while they only subscribed to capital stock to the extent of $11,000.00, they have put in, in the form of loans, some $55,000.00. There is something in all this which can almost surely be applied to our own tax benefit. Podoll and Lasser are thrashing it out now. Furthermore, they are still entitled to process about 35 tons of paper in 1943, which makes a sweet sound in my ears. Well, we'll see. Needless to say, Hal is not to be thrown in. On the contrary. That also goes for Durrell.

There are a few more possibilities in the offing, but these are the hot ones.

I enclose a full-page ad from the SRL on WINTER'S TALES. It is the basic ad of our campaign and has run in the Times, and will in the Trib. The book hasn't really gotten away heavily yet, but I think it will.

With all the best to you,

Yours,
Bennett

1943 JUN 13 PM 10 07

20 EAST 57 ST NYK=

AM ON TRIP PRETTY FAR FROM HOME AND POCA-
TELLO BACK TOMORROW BET LEW HAS NEVER
SOLD THIS TOWN LOVE=
DONALD.

June 15, 1943

Dear Don:

All of us were surprised to get your wire from Gulfport Field,
Miss. Why in hell didn't you steer that old crate up to La-
Guardia and drop in to dinner on your way back?

I hope that a copy of THIRTY SECONDS OVER TOKYO
was waiting for you by the time you got back to Pocatello. It
looks a little bit nebish at first glance, but once the public gets
used to the smaller sized book, I think they'll take it without a
murmur. Considine is delighted with it. We all met at a cocktail
party that Harry Maule gave for Jimmy Sheean on Friday, and
then saw Dick Tregaskis off on a clipper for Ireland. He expects
to be in on the invasion, and maybe we'll get another book out
of him just as successful as Guadalcanal. Both Tregaskis and
Considine are wonderful guys, and our whole relationship with
both of them has been an unalloyed pleasure.

Business continues on a very even keel. We are all just hanging
around holding our breaths for Tokyo to get away from the

barrier. Your old pal Adolph Kroch was just in oozing friend-ship from every pore. He left us an order for 3000 Modern Li-brary books.

Our social life is practically non-existent. We were down at the Schermans for the weekend, and are scheduled to go to George and Beatrice's [Kaufman] this next one, although I am going to get out of it if I can. These weekends this year are a God damn nuisance. The trains are hot and crowded for one thing, and the fact that you can't drive anywhere once you get to a place is an-other. My own idea of heaven is to lie around in my bathing trunks in our own back yard and get under the spray when it is hot. The unfortunate thing is that people just don't seem to understand this point of view, and get very hurt when we turn down their undoubtedly well-meant invitations. Beatrice, for instance, is going to be a problem. She acted a little bit miffy when I suggested that I'd be a hell of a lot happier having din-ner with them one evening in town.

Bob has been very wonderful during the last week and has won the undying devotion of everybody at Random House. That's about all I have to tell you except to repeat that I wish this God damn war was over, and that you were back here at Random House.

My love,
Bennett

June 16, 1943

Dear Bennett:

I couldn't resist sending you a telegram from Gulfport Miss. as it seemed so silly for me to be there. I decided to go on a planning mission for an overwater flight so Saturday morning at seven o'clock seven officers and two enlisted men set off for Gulfport in a B24E, as good a plane as there is but as uncomfortable as possible. There are so many guns and turrets and bombing devices that you bump your head every time you move. We flew at 20000' with oxygen smack over the Rockies past Denver and then came down to about 9000' and rode right in to Gulfport, arriving there at three in the afternoon with 700 gallons of gas left in the tanks. It's just short of 1600 miles, but we had no bombs so we could have gone on forever. Needless to say I was travelling with *three* good pilots so I wasn't taking any chances. Stayed in Gulfport Sunday, made all of our arrangements to run flights down there and then over the Gulf and flew back Monday. I flew the plane for a half hour and the boys in the back were so sick from my weaving around that they begged for mercy and we were 14 miles off course! It's like driving a damned Mack truck. Had lots of bad weather coming back, no visibility and snow storms thru' the mountains but it cleared miraculously as we hit Pocatello so we were able to come in. It really was a lot of fun and I learnt an enormous amount about the plane. You can't realize what four 1200 h.p. engines mean when they start turning over. The transports that we're used to just haven't half the power—but they have 1000 times the comfort. Now I'm thru' with flying for a while. I got a concentrated dose of it!

News beyond that, there is none. I'm managing to keep busy and not yet too bored but I wish to hell I could get out of here. Give my love to Bob and Pauline, Saxe, Lew & the gang. I wish I were with you.

When are you going away this summer? You're a sucker if you don't while business is good and you're able to.

Love to Thrup and Chris! Be good—

Love,
Donald

June 22, 1943

Dear Don:

Last night we sent you four dummies that may mark the beginning of a profitable and long-lived venture for us. The idea is an Illustrated Modern Library. Harry Abrams will be the art director of the project. In fact, the whole idea is his in the first place. I think he was pounding away at it even before he went into the Army, if I am not mistaken. Somebody is going to step into this field, and we might as well stake out a claim before it is too late. I am particularly wary on the subject of George Macy. His Heritage books are being marked at lower and lower prices every year. We certainly don't want any of his slimy hot breath on our necks!

The present plan is to bring out four or five of these Illustrated Modern Library editions for Christmas. We'll take the paper from our regular Modern Library stock and print token editions just so that we can be first in the field. Each book will be boxed. Some of them will be illustrated in color and some in black and white. The price will be either $1.25 or $1.45. The art work for each book will average us about $1000.00. After this expense is written off, the books will actually only cost us between 8¢ and

10¢ a copy more than the regular Modern Library. I am very anxious to hear your reaction to the idea. I think the dummies we've sent you are simply magnificent. They bowled over everybody who has seen them.

There is a lot of to-do about what titles we should select to start the series, but Confucius, Brothers Karamazov and Pickwick Papers will certainly be three of them. The other two will be selected from Don Quixote, Emerson, Longfellow, Candide, and Whitman. I am very anxious to have your opinion of all this.

Harry will be in on some sort of a royalty arrangement, possibly 3¢ a copy. He thinks he is going to make $20,000.00 a year out of it before many years have gone by, and I hope to hell he is right.

It is hotter than blazes around here today. Bob Haas went off to Vermont with Merle and the Schermans yesterday, so Jezebel and I have the Inner Sanctum entirely to ourselves today, and you can imagine what is going on. It's Jezebel's fourteenth wedding anniversary tomorrow. That guy Friedman is certainly a bear for punishment. (Jezebel says it is too hot to even protest against all these statements. That'll give you a rough idea of the weather.)

Cecil Brown is about to embark on a complete tour of the country and his next book will be a report on America. It might be big, and then again it might not. We can afford to lose a few thousand shekels on him, if necessary. Leane Zugsmith and Carl Randau have written a knockout mystery story which we'll probably sign up in the course of the next few days. We've tied up the INS man who is going to the Aleutians for a complete story of the war in that sector. LIFE WITH FATHER is ours for the Modern Library. It will be published in February 1944. That's all the news worth telling on a day like this.

How about calling up some night to say hello?

Love,
Bennett

June 26, 1943

Dear Bennett—

Your letter about the illustrated editions and the dummies arrived here this morning. I think they are really beautiful and I think the idea is fine. Harry and I had talked about the idea many times and I certainly think it's well worth doing some experimental work with them. Two words of advice on them. Nine point type is too small to be of enduring value in these books. Our printing is not careful enough to gamble setting even the larger books (longer works) in anything smaller than 9½ Fairfield and Fairfield is one helluva clear type. And look out for that inner margin of only ½ inch. These books are small and quite tightly bound and we don't want to make them hard to read. After all they are not really deluxe collectors items but books that will be used and we have to be careful of the *reading* quality as well as the looks. I'm most enthusiastic about these dummies and if we can keep our costs within reason at present inflated prices, we can use really good paper after the war and turn out some gems.

While we are making money and paying such high taxes have you and Bob thought of going into the college text field and possibly getting some men interested in that. I know it's lousy now but this might be the time to make a deal with some-one. Just a dream but not a new one.

Did you ever buy Smith & Durrell and did the Whitman deal go thru' for the Woolworth juveniles?

I received the 2 copies of Tokyo. I think the book itself is fine. I like its looks but I think the jacket is lousy. It's cheap and garish and not up to R.H. standards. So we should sell 250,000 copies. We've never had a real success with our best jackets. That's enough "bitching" for to-day but I know you want my honest opinion!

Have the final figures come thru' yet. I'd like to know what they are before write down, after write down, and the taxes, God bless 'em. I'm broke as a beaver and want to know that my R.H. interest is increasing by leaps and bounds!

Had the CO down for dinner last night, an old man of 27 from Guadalcanal, a Lt. Col. and a fine sensitive youngster. He's new at the field and I like him plenty. There's been no ex-citement around here. Two out of our four squadrons have gone off to combat as replacements so things are really pretty quiet, as the new news hasn't come in yet.

I still have no idea how long I'll be here—when I'll go to Or-lando and start the final trek out of the country. It will happen when I least expect it of that I'm sure.

It's lovely and cool here so I guess I should not complain. But I still prefer 20 East to Pocatello. And I don't trust you alone with my Pauline!

My love to all—

                                                                    Donald

Will return the dummies under sep. cover!

June 30, 1943

Dear Don:

There is a cool breeze blowing today and everybody is suddenly full of pep again. It marks the end of two weeks of the
most insufferable hot weather that I think New York has ever
known.

Saturday afternoon Harry Abrams, Lew Miller and Ray Freiman
came up to my house. The four of us put on bathing trunks and
sat around the back yard talking about the Illustrated Modern
Library for about two hours. Every few minutes we punctured
the conversation long enough to turn the hose on each other. It
was about 96 in the shade out there! I am enclosing herewith a
list of fifty titles that we selected for possible inclusion in the series when, as and if. I will be interested in hearing your comments on same. Note that all but one of them (The Bible) are
already in the Modern Library. The Bible project is to me the
most exciting thing connected with the whole affair to date.
LeRoy Baldridge is going to do decorations and some illustra-
tions for the job. We are having trial pages set now, and Harry
Abrams is sure that we can get the whole thing in about 1060
pages, Modern Library size. For the illustrated editions, we'll
use a second color tint block as background. Maybe you will remember the experimentation that was done with this device for
that BOMC–Random House Shakespeare that never came to
anything. That is the sort of thing we'll use on The Bible. For
our regular Modern Library, of course, we won't have the second color, but Baldridge is planning the work so that it will look
perfect in black and white. This will make volume No. 4 for the
Modern Library some time next year. Now all we need is a dictionary and our dream of having Shakespeare, The Bible and
the dictionary in the Modern Library will have come true. To

me this is about as important as anything that has been done by this firm since we started. And the beauty of it is that these terribly expensive plates are costing us so very little because of the tax situation.

Ah yes, the tax situation! After writing off everything we could possibly dream of in connection with both Random House and the Modern Library advances, and also deducting approximately $25,000.00 for the new pension fund, we still had a net profit of something like $412,000.00. Mannie, Abe and I then got to work on the good old inventory and managed to get the net figure down to $285,000.00, which is what I am afraid we are going to have to report. $25,000.00 of the inventory cut came off the Modern Library. We got that figure by reducing our present inventory to the same figure that we used last year. The rest of the cut came out of the Random House inventory. A large part of it, of course, is on our present stock of Duplaix books.

The Smith-Durrell deal fell through because Horace advised us that we'd be treading on very thin ice if we tried using their paper or apply their losses to our own tax problem. The literary properties weren't worth the paper that this letter is written on. . . . The Duplaix deal, however, is definitely set, and Georges was more optimistic yesterday about production than he has been in a long time. We may not get all the juveniles we want from him this Fall, but we are certainly going to get many thousand more than we counted on. We could sell ten times the number that we are getting. . . . We are also getting 100,000 pounds of paper extra from A.B. Barnes & Co. Hal Dunbar wangled this deal for us. This paper will take care of the entire run on the Illustrated Modern Library, and then some. . . . Early reports on TOKYO are nothing short of ecstatic. In this connection, I am enclosing letters from Knopf and Schuster. I think you will be amused at the difference between the really sincere man and a professional—and to me, obvious—soft soaper!

Jezebel says she now has to go to the can, so I will close with lotions of love.

Walter Winchell Cerf

P.S. Ed Falk has fallen for a Cuban dancer of 27 and will probably marry her. Sartorius is also in love. His gal is an Ensign in the Waves, and so far is holding out.

Incidentally, it may be a matter of mild interest to you to know that GUADALCANAL nudged gracefully over the 100,000 mark yesterday. First time in our history. And SUEZ is over 90,000. My present guess is that TOKYO will be over 200,000 before the end of the year.

July 4, 1943

Dear Bennett—

Boy—was it a pleasure to get your long and newsy letter. . . . It came on a particularly dreary day. July 4th and nothing to celebrate except being on the job as usual. My boss leaves for Mountain Home to-morrow on assignment I wouldn't wish on Hitler—and I will become the Group S2 [intelligence officer] as of to-morrow. This rates a majority and eventually I'll get it because they'll send me out of the country as a Group S2 not a Squadron. I got a big kick out of your enclosure from Lynn. I'm giving some of the same lectures over here and I, too, don't know a damned thing about the subjects. I don't envy Lynn his job—and I hope I don't get sent to England. They won't allow Intelligence officers to fly in the 8th Air Force. All the others insist on your flying some missions!

Congratulations on Guadalcanal going over 100,000. Tokyo will blanket it in two months I hope. The list of titles that you suggest for the illustrated books is swell, but some of our plates are pretty bad. If you use the ML plates have them checked pretty carefully. The Renoir, for instance, is a duplicate set of Burt plates and shouldn't be used for anything anymore. Also about using the Kents for Candide? . . . 37—174—199 are all pretty small and quite battered but the titles are grand. Quite a series of books you publish Mr. Cerf! I'm just as pleased about the Bible idea as you are. It's grand to do it and the present set up makes it damned near perfect.

How about a small illustrated book of the documents of democracy and our own history? The Articles of Confederation, Declaration of Independence, Constitution, Bill of Rights— something of Monroe Doctrine—Lincoln material, Emancipation Proclamation—Gettysburg Address—Wilson's inaugural and war message—F.D.R.'s first inaugural—Atlantic Charter etc. There's so much talk of what the hell this country stands for that an attractive 150-page book, possibly illustrated, gathered by some historian who knows the documents and would keep it short and simple might have a reasonable sale. Sort of the St. John's idea applied to American history. Going to the source rather than the interpretation. Nevin's or Commager would do a job! So throw the idea in the waste basket! . . .

The R.H. list doesn't look too strong for this fall but we'll be counting on Tokyo, I'm sure—if the 1944 list is good there's nothing to worry about but taxes. I hope to Christ Walter Clark's book is good. He's a good property.

A happy July 4th to you. I take it that Chris and Phyllis are
both blooming. Kiss Pauline for me, chastely, you bastard! My
love to Bob, Saxe and the gang—

As ever,
Donald

July 9, 1943

Dear Major-to-Be:

As I wired you yesterday, I was mighty happy to hear that you
had gotten the job that you've been angling for. Personally, I
prefer your getting a job that would keep you anchored close to
the ground right here in the United States, but obviously
you've got your fool heart set on something else and, knowing
what a stubborn bastard you are, I realize that nothing can be
done about it. Go ahead and get your ass shot full of ack-ack;
poor old Cerf will carry on in his usual faithful fashion at 20
East 57th Street. (Of course, you realize that "carry on" has several connotations!)

Monday is the official publication date for TOKYO. Of course
we're all holding our breaths to see if the public shares the un-
restrained enthusiasm of all the booksellers, critics and ourselves. Frankly, I don't see how the book can miss. Even that old
sourpuss Harold Williams called up to say, "Boy, what you
could do with that book if Klopfer were on the job!" I will keep
you closely posted on significant day-to-day sales in the first
fortnight.

In the meantime, another manuscript has arrived that kept me
bouncing up and down on the edge of my chair just the way

GUADALCANAL and TOKYO did. I begged King Features to find me something on the Aleutian campaign, and damned if those bastards didn't come across again. Some youngster named Howard Handelman has done 250 pages of the most wonderful war stuff imaginable. It hasn't been cleared by any of the censors yet and a lot of it, I am sure, is going to have to be taken out. Do you think it would be safe for me to mail it out to you to Idaho for a quick look-see? I have to have it back pronto since we have no copy, and I don't want to send it unless you are *absolutely sure* that it will be all right. Let me know about this. We cannot do anything with the book, of course, until the Kiska show is completed. Handelman is in San Francisco at the moment, but is leaving for the front next week. He has assurances that he will be there in time for anything spectacular. Even if we never get another word of the manuscript, what we have is good for a 50,000 minimum, I am sure. Where are we going to get the paper? How the hell do I know?

You may consider the Illustrated Modern Library officially launched. Horace is drawing up a contract with Harry Abrams which means that my eight line memo is now being elaborated into a 42-page document. We are paying 3¢ a copy royalty on the first 15,000 of any title and 5¢ a copy thereafter. Five titles are projected for this Fall and another ten for next year and Abrams, who moves faster than anybody I've ever seen, has got the fifteen most important artists in America all lined up already for the project. Included are Thomas Benton, Stewart Edward Curry, Edward Wilson, George Grosz, and several other top notchers whom a dope like you never heard of. (Me either. Besides, I can't remember them at the moment.) At any rate, I will send you a complete outline in a few days' time, as soon as we get it all put down on paper. The important thing, of course, is The Bible, and that's what everybody is concentrating on at the moment. If the other four titles don't get out this Fall, it will be a matter of little importance to us. The Bible, however, is going to be a wow. Under present market conditions, we could sell 100,000 of them, if we had them.

The big social news of the moment is that Phyllis' mother is arriving for the weekend tomorrow. Zowie! And to add further joy to my life, I have just heard that that slimy, ass-kissing son-of-a-bitch Silberberg has been made a Lieutenant Colonel. I can't state my full views of this situation since Jezebel has not yet reached that point in her education. Pfooey!

There is probably some other news around that would interest you, but enough is enough. Why don't you call up some evening?

Love to you and Pat.

As ever,
Bennett

July 11, 1943

Dear Bennett—

Thanks so much for your telegram with the good news of Tokyo reviews. 250,000 by Christmas is our goal and I really think we have a good chance of reaching it. I take it the advance was around 45 to 50,000! Send me something on the Aleutian book when you have a chance. I hope you're not kidding about its excellence.

I am no longer the Group S2. Two days after I took over a major from Command and Staff School came in here assigned to Intelligence. The CO practically threw him out on his ass but he came from higher authority so he had to be made the S2. I'm running the Dept. and am responsible for it, but I'm no longer the boss. So I suspect I'll be shipped out within a reasonable time! I really don't give a damn as what I want is my own combat group, and I know I'll get it eventually.

Life continues to run along at a smooth and pleasant pace. We're living comfortably and the weather is gorgeous, not working too hard, and my only complaint is a feeling of restlessness and futility.

Give my love to Bob, Thrup and the office in general. Am holding my thumb for Tokyo!

Love,
Donald

1943 JUL 12 PM 6 20

BENNETT A CERF

TRANSFERRED TO FOUR FORTY FIFTH BOMBARD-
MENT GROUP SIOUX CITY IOWA LEAVING TOMOR-
ROW. GOOD BREAK LETTER FOLLOWS ADDRESS
MAIL ARMY AIR BASE ABOVE ADDRESS LOVE=
DONALD.

July 13, 1943.

CAPTAIN DONALD S. KLOPFER
445th BOMBARDMENT GROUP
SIOUX CITY, IOWA

WELCOME AND GOOD LUCK   EAGERLY AWAIT
DETAILS   LAWSON A RUNAWAY

BENNETT

July 17, 1943

Dear Cerfie—

Many thanks for your wire of welcome which I picked up as I reported in at the Base this morning. How far has Tokyo gone? The word runaway in your telegram made me feel mighty good.

We had a fine trip from Pocatello here. Spent the first night in Jackson and then went thru' Yellowstone, "Old Faithful" performing on schedule and effectively—then the Shoshone National Park in Wyoming. Spent the night in a motel at Sheridan, Wyoming, and into South Dakota visiting the Rushmore Memorial and spending the night in Chamberlin, S.D. on the Missouri River. Then across corn and wheat and into Sioux City last night. A good trip but it's hotter than hell in this hole now.

I reported out at the Base this morning. The 445th is an Operational Training Unit in the middle of first phase training. So I should be here for about three months and then go over with this outfit. I'm the boss of the Intelligence Section, have a good

CO and Operation's Officer, so from now on it's up to me! Things are pretty rugged here now, but I think they can be straightened out pretty soon. This setup is not as clean as Pocatello was—really nearer field conditions. That's really all I know about it so far—will write more when I know more.

Pat and Tony are still with me. She'll look for an apartment to-morrow. In the meantime, we're comfortable here.

My love to Bob, Saxe, Lew, Pauline and the gang at large. I'd still rather be at 20 East than here!

Love,

Donald

July 20, 1943

Dear Don:

I just received your welcome letter telling me of your safe arrival in Sioux City. I don't like your happy chortle over the prospect of getting overseas so soon, but if that's what you want, what the hell can I do to stop you?

We're in a state of suspended animation over TOKYO. The advance sale was enormous and the reviews couldn't have been better; now we've got to wait until the advance stock is consumed and the real reorders start pouring in. Yesterday's total was 1166, but 1000 of this was one order from the Infantry Journal. The stores all report that the book is off to a wow of a start. I am sure we have nothing to worry about, but it's sort of tantalizing to sit around here waiting for the anticipated rush of reorders. Due to vacations, sicknesses, resignations and whatnot, the sales chart is now a full two weeks behind, so I can't give you an exact figure on the book to date. It seems to me that it is somewhere around 55,000. That may be off a couple of thousand in either direction.

Meanwhile, the wonder of the ages is GUADALCANAL. The total for that one on Friday was 965 copies, and it is a rare day when the sales don't reach 200. I think we are up to about 105,000 now. What a gold mine this book has been. The other books are holding up well too, and it is hard to remember that these are the mid-summer doldrums!

I take it that you received a copy of Podoll's annual report showing the net of about $255,000.00 that I told you about. . . . Meanwhile, as usual, my dear Klopfer, we don't seem able to get our paws on a God damn cent of all these mythical riches. Anyhow, we are getting some wonderful plates: Shakespeare, The Bible, Aquinas, and God knows what else. Furthermore, we are gradually going to replace the worn out plates in the Modern Library. I am just finishing a completely new collection of ghost stories to replace that stinking old No. 73, and Aaron Sussman is working on a revision of the de Maupassant volume. Did you ever look into that one? It is really disgraceful. A new LEAVES OF GRASS and the PEPYS DIARIES are also on the calendar.

I am curious to know how you and Pat liked my piece on Gershwin in the Saturday Review. Maybe you missed it in all your jumping around. I am sending you a duplicate copy under separate cover.

I am hot, annoyed with the mass of detail work that has been around, temporarily sick of the publishing business. Phyllis, Christopher, the nurse and I are going down to stay with Alicia for two weeks beginning July 30th, and I will be glad to get away. Harry [Guggenheim], incidentally, is now a full-fledged Commander and his field at Trenton is in operation. All the new Navy planes are brought to his field and it is there that the secret Navy devices are installed. It is a very responsible job and he is having the time of his life doing it.

I suppose you saw that Johnny Swope married Dorothy Maguire of Claudia; that John Anderson and Colonel Little of Little & Ives passed on during the last week; and that Alfie Knopf has bought Pen Publishing (for tax purposes, I will vow). Manges is 45 today and Sartorius will be 50 tomorrow. Time, if I may coin a phrase, passes on.

My deep love to you.

As ever,
Bennett

July 22, 1943

Dear Bennett—

Both Pat and I thought your Gershwin article was swell. With typical Selwyn press agent soul she only sniffed once and said, "Gertie Lawrence became a star in Charlot's Review?"! But really, both of us liked it. I hadn't seen it because the SRL usually gets lost between Santa Ana, Harrisburg, Pocatello and here. Anyway we found out to-day that we're staying here for the month of August. That's preferable to the plains of Nebraska.

The business figures sound great. I saw the prelim P & L statement and hope you can chisel something off our tax. I'd like a little backlog when we come out of this mess. Don't get discouraged because Tokyo reorders aren't in yet. It takes time in the month of July to eat up a 50000 advance. September is when it should start ramping and it ought to lead the best sellers during the fall. It would be perfectly safe to send me that Aleutian manuscript, registered mail, if you can spare it for a week. I'll keep it in the safe and return it to you by registered mail if you so desire. I'm delighted that we're making new plates of the ML's. God knows they need it! I hope you stay down at Alicia's with the family for a while. Don't let the business get you down. It's so much pleasanter than any other business in the world. And that includes any job in the AAF!

The setup here is fine. Lt. Col. Terrill is the CO, a helluva flier and a good fellow. Our Operations officer is a honey and the executive is a stinker, but there are no complaints. We're slow getting started because there seems to be a bottleneck in first phase training whence we draw our crews.

Incidentally, time marches on! I'm the oldest man in the 445th Bomb troop (H)!

My love to all the office, Phyllis and Chris.—

Love,
Donald

July 28, 1943

Dear Don:

We've just gotten the Army and Navy okay on the Aleutian manuscript and are going to shove it right into composition. Don't you want to wait until we get proofs to send you? If not, I can send you a carbon copy of the manuscript, but it is in a

pretty cheesy state. Let me know which you prefer. There is
nothing of a startling news nature in the book, and if I were
you, I'd wait to read it comfortably. It is just wonderful war re-
porting. Incidentally, I have high hopes of selling a hunk of it
to Readers Digest for a pre-publication feature. Ralph Hender-
son of the Digest spent Monday night at my house reading the
script. He was very deeply impressed. It is just a matter of room
with those babies now.

Incidentally, they have started an Arabic edition in addition to
the Spanish, Portuguese and Swedish ones. The French one is
on tap. Boy, what power that outfit is going to be able to wield
all over the world by the time it gets finished. It is a little worri-
some to think about!

I am enclosing herewith a one-color proof of the double-page
ad we are going to run in Publishers Weekly on the Illustrated
Modern Library. Next week I hope to have some real dummies
to send you. Harry Abrams and Ray Freiman have collaborated
to do a wonderful job on these books, and I really think you are
going to be excited with the results.

The corrected proofs of the Fall Random House announcement
are going back to Bill Simon. I have finished my Trade Winds
column all the way through August and on Friday night I sign
off for two weeks. Our address for the first two weeks of August
will be c/o Commander Harry Guggenheim, Port Washington,
L.I. Jezebel will also be away the first three weeks in August.
(That's what life is like these days. The boss gets two weeks and
the hired help gets three.) The title of the Random House office for the next few weeks will be "Sex Takes a Holiday."

Ted Lawson spent the night with us last night. Hollywood
hasn't spoiled him at all. He will stay in Washington for two

weeks and then shove off for his new post in Chile. The book is romping along nicely but is not yet the sensation that we hoped for. These are the dog days, however, and no book is doing anything wonderful at the moment.

Tonight we are going with Jake Wilk of Warner Bros. to see the opening of THIS IS THE ARMY. It ought to be pretty swell. Tomorrow we have a date with old Schloppo. He and Phyllis are putting the finishing touches to a really fine anthology called TALES OF TERROR AND THE SUPERNATURAL. They have worked like slaves on it and the result is so good that I honestly think we have a good chance of selling it to the Book-of-the-Month Club as a dividend. I am going to take this up with Harry Scherman as soon as I get back from Long Island.

That seems to be about all the news. Take care of yourself and keep me posted on your activities. Judging by the headlines of the last few days my prediction that you will be back at your desk here by January 1, 1945, does not sound too impossible. Anyway, I can have my dreams.

As ever,
Bennett

Aug. 1, 1943

Dear Bennett—

. . . As of to-morrow everyone is being restricted to the Base. We have one helluva training program to meet and the Colonel very sensibly is impressing it on all officers and men.

That means 24 hours off per week and I don't think it will last too long. Pat's moving to the Sioux Apt which will be like a girls dormitory. There are so many Army wives living there. I don't know how long she'll stick it out under these new conditions.

The war certainly is going along at a great clip these days. I'd hate like hell to be living in Harrisburg now! I'm sure the Italians will quit any minute now. They're in a hopeless spot.

I certainly am jealous of you lazying around down at Alicia's for a couple of weeks. I'll get six days before I go over—don't know when I'll take them, imagine some time in Sept.

I hope you're right about Jan. 1, 1945, but I don't believe it for a minute! Give my love to Thrup and Chris—and remember me to the Guys—

Love,
Donald

August 9, 1943

Dear Don:

I came in for just the day to take care of an accumulation of letters and junk of one sort or another. We have had a wonderful week at Alicia's and I am going back for some of the same on a late train this afternoon. The weather has been superb, and good old George Abbott brings around a different beautiful girl for tennis every afternoon. He also had Frank Sinatra out last Thursday, which caused all the women in the vicinity to swoon with delight. Personally I preferred Joan Caulfield who is the star of his KISS AND TELL company, and who is really a knockout. Harry came back from Trenton for the weekend, and we had a fine time despite the presence of Doctor Al Barach who is fuller of crap than ever. Freddy, incidentally, sends you her love, and so do the Guggenheims.

Chris took country life right in his stride, although the Sound has proved a little too big for him, to date. When I lift him over the water, he pulls in his legs just like an airplane taking in its wheels after it hits the air. He is beginning to talk a blue streak, but most of the time I haven't got the faintest idea of what he's saying. Phyllis says I am a neglectful parent.

I find that business is sailing along at a terrific clip. TOKYO is at last beginning to show signs of real life. It's way up on all the best seller lists in the Times compilation this morning. As you say, no war book has been able to compete with the front page headlines in the past couple of weeks.

By way of diversion, I am writing the editorials for Alicia's newspaper while I am down there. It's wonderful fun to be able to shoot your mouth off without having to sign your name to your spoutings. For tomorrow morning's paper I prove conclusively that Germany can't last another six months. I am sure this will cheer you up immeasurably.

Oppenbopper writes that he's coming to town for a week and will honor us by staying with us during that time. We will be glad to see him—but I wish it were you instead. I hope that everything is working out just the way you want it. Please send me all the details, if you can.

Love,
Bennett

P.S. I had a long letter from Bobby Heller this morning. The s.o.b. is in Sicily. And oh yes, Irving Fineman is coming to the office tomorrow morning. That's why I am beating it back to Port Washington this afternoon.

Aug. 18, 1943

Dear Bennett,

I suppose by this time you've practically forgotten that you were off on a vacation for a couple of weeks—but, what the hell, Random House is more fun than a vacation anyway!

I've been granted my leave and I expect to be in N.Y. by the 8th of Sept. returning here the 14th. A short time but that's all they'll give us these days. Needless to say I'm most anxious to see you and Bob and the gang again—to say nothing of Lois and my Ma!

The training program here is clicking at a great rate. We're working on a 24 hour schedule and really putting in a helluva lot of flying hours. My Intelligence Dep't is so busy briefing and interrogating that the boys are running in circles. I seem to thrive in it and since I'm the oldest man in the group the youngsters have to really step along to keep up.

Pat's having a lousy time—comes out every evening to a bad dinner out here and then goes home around ten thirty—not such a pleasant life. But she insists upon sticking around, so more power to her.

There isn't a damned bit of news around here except local gossip.

Has 30 Seconds started to really roll yet and what are the figures? Anything exciting for the fall?

My best to Chris and Thrup.

Love,
Donald

August 20, 1943

Dear Don:

I just this moment received your letter, and I am delighted that you are going to be here from the 8th to the 14th. God knows it's a short enough time, but it's better than nothing. Is there any chance of you and Pat staying with us those days? I needn't tell you that we would love to have you, and that if you came you would be under no obligation whatever to spend any more time with us than you wanted to. Please think about it anyhow. Frankly, if I were in your place, I think I would want the biggest suite at the Waldorf for those six days to wallow in Sybaritic luxury—but you were never as much a creature of the flesh as I am, and maybe 132 East 62nd Street will be good enough for you. Do let me know.

Second, how about saving Thursday evening, September 9th, for Phyllis and me, whether or not you stay with us. I know you will be beset with engagements, and I would love to get in a claim before your various relatives and whatnots start tearing you apart. If you say the word, I will get tickets for one of the new shows, though God knows nothing new that's worth a God damn has come to town in months.

. . .

The news on TOKYO is not particularly good. It's selling, yes, but nothing like what we thought it would, and I am more convinced than ever that the bloom is off the rose on the war babies. I should say that the total to date is somewhere around 56,000 or 57,000. With a break, we will hit about 75,000 before the year is over, in my opinion, and that will just about clean us out of the edition, since we have given 22,000 of our 100,000 to the Book-of-the-Month Club. Six months ago I still think that this book would have sold a quarter of a million copies at least. It certainly is a tough break for Mr. Morgenthau.

Between ourselves, I regard the Fall list as minor league or New York Giants calibre. The Aleutian book, which I hope you have read by this time, is a pip, but after our experience with TOKYO we are only printing an edition of 15,000, and I am in hopes we will run the sale up to 25,000, but further than that I don't think we will be able to go. WHERE'S SAMMY? looks like a reasonable 8,000 to 10,000 shot, and that goes for Lewis Browne's novel, too. Harry Maule's BOOK OF WAR LETTERS is a question mark. The real dark horse on the list is ROSTOV. I just sold condensation rights to Liberty for $1,000.00 which is a good send-off for the book anyhow. I think I told you that Readers' Digest has bought the Aleutian book. Our share of this sale will be a minimum of $1,000.00 and may amount to considerably more. Incidentally, Readers' Digest has definitely decided to make a regular department of the Trade Winds column. The present plan is to run a double page feature of excerpts from the column every other month, and to alternate this with the same length extract from the New Yorker's Talk of the Town. Needless to say, I am pretty tickled. They have also bought the Gershwin piece from me, so I will be rolling in wealth until the next tax payment comes along.

. . .

The big news of the week was handed to me by Georges Duplaix yesterday afternoon. He came in to tell us that he was resigning from Western to become graphic arts editor of Simon & Schuster. Graphic arts my left blank, says I. If I may be permitted to hazard a guess (try and stop me), those bastards are going to crack the chain store market within the next two years. Octopi, that's what they are, Klopfer, octopi. I am meeting Mr. Benbow at 4:30 this afternoon to talk over the situation with him and see who's going to take Duplaix's place. As long as they keep Lucille Ogle, I think we will manage, but there's no gainsaying the fact that the loss of Duplaix is a kick in what we Oxford boys used to call the arse.

Speaking of octopi, the finished dummies on the illustrated Modern Library are absolutely terrific, and I only wish I could see that poop George Macy's puss when he gets his first look at them. Take my tip and sell a couple of hundred shares of Heritage Press short at the market.

We had a really spectacular time down at Alicia's. Christopher gained almost two pounds while we were there. The last night of our visit was highlighted by the presence of [her father] Captain Patterson and Ruth Vischer. I had promised Alicia that I would be Joe Charm as long as her pappy was about, and not start any controversial arguments. I was so wonderful that the nearest we came to a clash was a brief discussion on the relative merits of Christy Mathewson and Three-Fingered Brown.

Bob Haas has gone to camp. I hope it will do him some good. He's lost about fifteen pounds since Bob Junior died, and looks like hell.

The only other news I can give you from the office is that Jezebel is away until Monday, which leaves me absolutely nobody to potch. On the other hand, I am having lunch Monday with Anne Baxter so I won't complain.

My love to you, and I hope you will be able to stay with us. Don't forget the central location: Mama Jacobson on one side and Mama Goldsmith on the other. Yippee!

> As ever,
> Bennett

Aug. 23, 1943

Dear Bennett—

Thanks for your letter and your invitation to stay at the house. We're going to stay at the Beekman as all of Pat's clothes etc. are there and the Goldsmiths are still down in the country. Thursday night would be fine for us. If there's no show the four of us can dine and sit around and chew the fat. I'm going to try to spend Wednesday night with Bob and Merle and I feel sure that they'll want to see me as I haven't spoken to Bob since Bob Jr's death. I do hope this camp session does him some good. He must look awful if he's lost fifteen pounds.

There is one thing that you could do for me. Since Goldsmith's is not really open I'm stuck without a place to have those people in to say good-bye that I think I *should* see, for Pat's sake as well as my own. If you could have the enclosed list of people in to your house after dinner Monday night—the 13th—it would save me a helluva lot of trouble. It would be the most ghastly party as such that I could imagine but my good Jewish conscience says that I should at least have a drink with them. And it would save tearful good-byes from my Mother etc. I'd be delighted to pay for it and you could have a caterer in to save wear and tear on the servants. I hate to ask this of you but there's no one else that I can ask. If you have some other plans made let me know and I'll ask Mother to do it—but I don't know how large her place is or whether it's even settled yet. But, honestly, Bennett, my feelings won't be hurt if you don't want to start anything with that bunch of clucks!

Planes have been grounded for two days for inspection so things have been dull around here. It looks as tho we should go overseas around the middle of Oct. but you can never tell.

Congrats on the Readers Digest Deal—you're a famous and wealthy guy now! Me, I'm broke and chomping at the bit to get this training period over with!

My love to Thrup, Chris—and kiss Jezebel for me.

Love,
Donald

August 25, 1943

Dear Donald:

Of course we'll have the party for you on Monday night, September 13th. Will you please rush me the addresses of the Feiners, the Kingsleys, Fanny Goldsmith, the Hundleys, Newmans, Hilsons, Harrises, and Edward Pullmans. I suppose I could find most of them in the telephone book, but some of them may still be away for the summer and Pat will know their present addresses at the drop of a hat. I am particularly concerned about where we'll find Fanny Goldsmith. She called up the other night to say that she was on her way to Pittsburgh to join Bert who, as I am sure you know, is a Captain being trained for

AMGOT* (and did you know that AMGOT is the Turkish word for horse manure?).

Also, would you like to have anybody like the Cecil Browns at the party, and would you like me to ask Saxe and Lew? I won't do anything about this until I hear from you, and Jez will not make a carbon of this letter so Saxe and Lew won't know anything about it if you think they wouldn't quite fit into this little grouping.

Don't forget that we have a foursome date for Thursday night. I won't get tickets until the last minute because, unless something really good comes along, I think it will be much more fun to linger over the dinner table and have a quiet evening together. I will write to the other people on the list immediately inviting them for about 9:30 or 10. Don't worry about the details. It will be my great pleasure to attend to them.

Where do you get that stuff about "being broke"? You are making more money every day than you ever dreamed you would have in a lifetime. Of course, there is a slight catch in that you can't lay your hands on a cent of it, but the thought should at least be gratifying. There was another Navy order last week for about 12,000 Modernlibes, followed by another from the Army today for the same quantity. The Army order also included 500 Gideon, 500 Tokyo, 500 Wisdom of China, and about a dozen other items, several of which have been out of print for about a year. The whole business is becoming sort of ludicrous.

F. Hugh Herbert was in yesterday. He is the author of KISS AND TELL and, as I am sure we told you, we are going to publish his Corliss Archer stories in book form next year. He is just

*American Military Government of Occupied Territory.

doing a special scenario job for one of the big studios and is being paid $2000.00 a week for it. Since he is now in the 96% bracket, he is keeping out of this 2000 bucks exactly $80.00 every week. This is the guy who was making $150.00 in all just one year ago. What a business!

I just had a drink with Anne Baxter. Since Jezebel has come back from her vacation she has taken to wearing some kind of iron underwear, so I thought it high time that I explored some new territory. (Jezebel is looking annoyed.)

It is still very hot and if I hadn't had two frozen daiquiris within the past hour, I probably wouldn't be in such good spirits. It will be great seeing you. The office is on the verge of hysteria. Please let me know exactly when you will arrive and how. If possible, I will meet you with the wartime equivalent of a brass band.

Love,
Bennett

Sept. 17, 1943

Dear Bennett—

I had a most uneventful trip back but a five hour layover in Omaha made me get in at 2-15 in the morning. I saw the CO at eight o'clock and at 10 I was on my way to Gulf Port Miss. in a B24. Remained there overnight and was back here last night. Three days in the air is too much for a man of my tastes. I don't like flying that much.

We've received our mission orders for Oct. 1, but the lot is still fighting for an extension until at least the 15th. I'm to go over with the advance party, the CO, S3, Communications Officer and myself. That means two crack pilots and a nice new ship so that's agreeable to me, but when we'll leave, I don't know. If we don't get an extension we should go to-day—but that's set! The Col. has a habit of getting what he's after so I think he'll succeed.

Again thanks for your party—Due to Phyllis' and your kindness and graciousness it was much better than I anticipated. I can't tell you how much I appreciate it. And don't ever worry about anything coming between us. Nothing can and nothing will and that goes for wives, children or mistresses! I was delighted to find you well and contented and going ahead with your writing. It's good stuff and please don't get lazy with it again.

My very best to the office gang. I was sorry to leave them all. I'd like to pitch in and work, but I guess I have a full time job on my hands now!

All love,
Donald

Sept. 24/43

Dear Bennett—

. . . I've been out at the Satellite field all week—up at five every morning—that combined with Gulf Port last week has gotten me pretty tired out. There's an air of expectancy around here now—we are so definitely on the last lap that I'm sure our orders will be changed at the last minute. I expect to be leaving some time in the first week of October with the advance party.

I should have some time to get adjusted wherever we're going before the mob comes in.

News, other than work, is absolutely nonexistent—you might get a phone call from me any day now that I'm on my way to the 21st Wing which is our staging area.

My love to Bob, Phyllis and the whole gang—

Love,
Donald

September 27, 1943

Dear Klopf:

I am delighted to know that we may at least get a chance to talk to you on the phone before you shove off. Make the call if you possibly can!

Don't be too bearish on that new list. I told you it didn't sound like much on paper, but there is gold in those hills. A couple of them are going to come through in a big way, I am sure. Furthermore, Quent Reynolds just blew in with three-quarters of a new manuscript, which is what we boys call gelt in the bank. And Elliot wrote us the title of his new Homer Evans story. He is calling it MURDER HE SAYS. I think it's a pip. Furthermore, I just sold Twentieth Century-Fox a thousand copies of the BOMC JANE EYRE at a net cash profit to Random House of 506 bucks. You and Pat can have a champagne supper at least on your share of that downright gift.

Thrup and I spent the weekend with the Schermans, where two chairs collapsed under me, Harry ripped his best pair of pants on a protruding nail in the living room, and Bernadine discovered on Sunday morning that there weren't any eggs in the house. Major Bill Walling was also in attendance. He is leaving tomorrow for Orlando, and expects to be overseas inside of two weeks. I never saw anything go so fast. He is in the Intelligence branch of the Air Corps and is working on some secret scheme that he himself devised which will take him clean around the world, he figures, in the next three months.

Business continues wonderful. Everything is smooth as silk except that God damn girdle of Jezebel's. I expect to lick this situation before Christmas.

My love,
Bennett

October 18, 1943

Dear Donald:

I have just received your note of October 14th. You know without my telling you everything I wish for you and how terribly happy I will be to see you back at your old desk again. But I thought I'd write you this note anyhow.

Write as often as you can. All good luck—and my deepest love.

As ever,
Bennett

APO 634-2 POSTMASTER N.Y.C.
OCT. 26, 1943

Dear Bennett—

I've been travelling around the countryside the past few days, seeing various and sundry bases and getting a birds eye view of what my job is to be in the near future. It's a good prospect and I think I'll have a lot of fun and excitement out of it.

I haven't yet seen anyone that I know over here, but I hope to get down to London one of these days and see some of the publishing poops altho there are not very many that it would be fun to see.

There's nothing to do on the Base so I expect to catch up on lots of reading that I've missed so far in my life. I'll be educated if I stay over here long enough. I certainly miss you like the devil, but to-night your bet about my return looks wrong by about a year instead of two years. My love to Thrup and, of course, yourself.

Donald

October 27, 1943

Dear Donald:

Pat called up to tell us that you were safe and happy and well. That news spread around the office faster than a report that the Book-of-the-Month Club had taken another of our books which, incidentally, they haven't.

Nothing very startling has happened since you shoved off . . . Chris is well again after a nasty siege of trench mouth and the

whole Sales Department is down at KMV [Warehouse] helping
to get out freight shipments (so now we are only two weeks behind), and yesterday's orders for SEE WHAT I MEAN totalled
exactly 5770 copies. Isn't it ridiculous? We could sell 100,000
of this book between now and Christmas—if we could get
them in the first place, and if we could ship them in the second.
Actually, we may get the total up to about 35,000, which ain't
hay.

I hope you are going to be able to tell us something of what you
are up to on the other side. Will you get to London for any
weekends? If so, I take it you will see Lynn Farnol, Beddington,
Plummer and all the rest. In case you've forgotten, the two publishers worth seeing are Jamie Hamilton and Harold Raymond
at Chatto & Windus. Give them all my love, please, if you do
run into them, and write soon.

I miss you something terrible.

As ever,
Bennett

Nov. 5, 1943

Dear Bennett,

Writing to you from the vast loneliness of the outskirts of
Merrie Englande is like thinking of another world. Strange as it
may seem my primary interest these days is that we had one
helluva lot of bombers over Germany yesterday. To-day, and
to-morrow! You lose your sense of proportion around a place
like this. I've been around at other bases which are now operat-

ing and have gotten my kick out of it occasionally. I don't know when I'll be able to get down to London if this pace keeps up and I hope to God it keeps up because then we'll all be home much sooner. If we can really paste those boys while the Russians are doing the real job it won't last forever! I'm well and happy here—reasonably comfortable in this cold climate—and hungry for news of yourself and of Random House.

Give my very best love to Bob and your Thrup and kiss Pauline for me—but in a gentlemanly way, you bastard, not like that!

Love,

Donald

Nov. 7, 1943

Dear Cerfie—

Thanks for your letter of the 27th. It was grand to hear from you—even the news of See What I Mean was good. I take it from your letter that we actually cannot manufacture the books. The paper supply has really run out and we're finally faced with the horrible thought of missing a best seller because we couldn't manufacture. That's war, my boy—maybe it will still be going big in 1944!

I almost froze my well known balls off last night. It was cold as all get out. The wind was blowing right thru' the damned Nissen Hut. The blankets seemed insufficient and the damned ack-ack kept me awake. But to-day, since I was ordered to go to church with 4 other officers to represent the AAF on Armistice Day which the churches celebrate to-day!— I was warmed by the hot air of a High Episcopalian minister.

To write of what I am doing is to write of very little. I'm still going around to bases to see what the score is in Intelligence and I'm trying to set up my department against what seems like impossible supply odds. Give me some good WPA workers rather than the labor they have around here. When I really settle down to doing a real job around here I'll feel much better. But I'm sure we won't be here forever. The Russians are winning the war for us!

Let me know what's happening. It's pretty lonesome around here. My best to Bob. Glad Chris has recovered.

Tell the sales force that if they're working at KMV it's the first honest work they've done in a long time.

Best love,
Donald

November 17, 1943

Dear Klops:

As Pat will no doubt write you, she went with us last night to see a prevue of Ginger Rogers in LADY IN THE DARK, and passed on the cheering news that the sun was actually shining in Britain and that you seemed to be thoroughly acclimated. Irita Van Doren, Belle Rosenbaum, Merle Haas and Bob and Herbert went to the prevue with us. The whole picture is in technicolor and is very swell, I think. It will make millions. We are selling the reprint rights of the play to World Books, so we'll get a little bit of the gravy anyhow. Stimulated by the prevue, we then moved on to the PRINCESS O'ROURKE at the Strand, and deposited your bride at the hotel at 2 A.M. She was so exhausted by all these goings-on that she agreed with me on two (2) arguments that came up in the latter part of the evening. Both of us were so astonished that we practically fell out of the taxicab. I must say that she looked very handsome last night.

The September P&L statement came in yesterday and is slightly unbelievable. The net figures for that month just about equal the total amount of your original investment in the Modern Library. For the first five months of the year we have written off the entire Shakespeare project and the entire first five volumes of the Illustrated Modernlibe. The net profit still shows slightly over 300 grand. Mr. Morgenthau must be very pleased with us. That "awful" Fall list that we were moaning about now shows SEE WHAT I MEAN over 30,000, EYE-LASHES over 45,000, ROSTOV over 13,000, and BRIDGE TO VICTORY over 12,000. The last seems to be building fast. WHERE'S SAMMY got a big puff from Winchell this morning. The advance is about 6000 and the movie sale is brewing with Fox. We get a cut of that. Incidentally, GUADALCANAL DIARY is a big hit in book form. Cartmell has already sold 150,000 copies of the dollar edition, with another 50,000 on press. As you can see, all these figures are so fantastic that they just don't mean anything any more. Despite all the prosperity, the publishers had their annual meeting yesterday and everybody cried a great deal more than usual. I was so damned bored that I walked out in the middle of Malcolm Johnson's speech thereby probably disgracing Random House forever and ruining your chances of being elected to the Publishers Lunch Club.

I am crazy to hear as many details as you are allowed to tell us of your activities in England. Write as often as you can and know that we are all missing you like hell and talking about you at a minimum of twenty times a day.

As ever,
Bennett

Nov. 20, 1943

Dear Bennett—

Thanks for your note with the news of Georgie's assignment to India. I must say that I'm rather jealous of him myself—that's much nearer what I wanted to do than the Eighth Air Force—but beggars can't be choosers. My CO arrived here this week and I am now firmly ensconced in his quarters—he, the Operations Officer and I are occupying three bedrooms, a living room and bath—with the usual inadequate heat but much better accommodations than I dared hope for on this side of the Atlantic. I went to school for three days last week and had dinner in London with Lynn Farnol now a Lt. Col. with the 8th Fighter Command Hq. He seems reasonably happy with his job—very happy with his promotion which completely wipes out the business of the phoney arrows. We dined together and sat around the Savoy Bar until 10-30 when we both went home. Saw Harold Raymond at Chatto—the next morning—no good books from them—he complains of a big bank balance and no books—spoke to Jamie [Hamilton, publisher] who was at the Ministry of Information but won't see him till I get down again. Met George Jones of Harpers, remember? who is a Lt. Col. at 8th Bomber Command—I guess I'm just a schlemiel but for some strange reason I don't envy those fellows at Hq. I like working right here in the Group with the crews themselves. I guess maybe I'm not ambitious, but I get more satisfaction out of helping some dumb flier than I would out of planning things in a higher echelon. So I guess this is where I'll stay!

I do hope that you're not too serious about envying us over here—things are just as piddling here as in the publishing business of that you may be sure—and John Macoy Jr. would be a whopping success in the Army! So don't think other people's pastures are greener—they aint! You do a good job with Random House and you'll contribute more to the good of the world than Oppenbopper, Klopfer and Mountbatten put together! Amen.

Let me hear what's happening at home. My best love to Bob and Thrup and, of course, yourself!

Love,
Donald

December 1, 1943

Dear Donald:

In the happy event that this note reaches you before Christmas please be assured that everybody in the office from top to bottom will be thinking of you and toasting you in the egg nog which we sincerely trust good old Miller will provide for the occasion. I am sure you know this without my telling you.

I received a note this morning from Lynn Farnol saying that he had seen you. I observe that he is now a Lt. Colonel, which sounds like very good going to me. All of us are hoping we'll get a long letter from you soon telling us exactly what is cooking in your department—or at least as much as you can safely say. Business continues wonderful, although there is nothing particularly new to tell you that's happened since the last time I wrote. Clare Jaynes' new book has been bought by Good Housekeeping for 7500 bucks. It will keep the wolf away from the starving little girls' door for a while.

Moss Hart's WINGED VICTORY is a terrific smash hit and I think we'll clean up on the book version. We've already sent you a copy and hope that it will get through to you. We've snagged Wolcott Gibbs away from Dodd Mead. I don't suppose he will ever be a great best seller, but he certainly is one of the slickest writers in the country and, besides, I know that you would want the husband of Mrs. Gibbs to be on the Random House list.

Personally, no special news at all. Thrup and I played bridge for the first time in six months the other night with the Bauers and got right into mid-season form by having a violent fight over the very first hand. For the rest, we are working hard and seeing the same old people night after night. God damn it, I'd like to get out of this rut. Hurry up and win the war and come back home where you belong.

My deep love,
Bennett

December 10, 1943

Dear Don:

Your letter dated November 20th arrived yesterday morning, and the one dated November 7th arrived today. If this keeps up, along about January 10th we ought to get a notice with a little pink ribbon on top announcing your birth—a black day, I may add, for civilization in general and Manhattan virginity in particular.

I am very glad that you were able to see some of the London publishing gentry and hope that it proved a pleasant interlude. Wouldn't it be nice you could uncover a great best seller and win the war simultaneously? If Jamie Hamilton has anything important up his sleeve, I count on you to get your lily white hands upon it.

The hectic pace of the last few months seems to have let up a little bit for the nonce. And a good thing too, because the nerves of all of us have been on the ragged edge. We solved our paper problems on both SEE WHAT I MEAN and YOU'RE SITTING ON MY EYELASHES. In fact, we may have solved them on the Lewis Browne book a little too well because we've got about 8000 copies in stock now and the demand has fallen off. I am going to try to goose Winchell into giving the book another plug on the air next week. WHERE'S SAMMY and BRIDGE TO VICTORY have done fine. SAMMY sold out its first printing of 8000 and we are well into a second run of 2000. We printed 15,000 BRIDGE and will be sold out on that edition by the end of next week.

I am sure somebody has written you already about the fact that last week's orders included over 60,000 Modern Library for the

Navy and over 13,000 for the Army. The Modern Library is zooming along on all six. As far as new authors are concerned, we've pried Allen Chase, author of FALANGE, away from Putnam's, Wolcott Gibbs from Dodd Mead, and Frances Crane, whose detective stories sell about as well as Dorothy Disney's, away from Lippincott. That will make up for the loss of Gene Fowler to Viking and old stinkpot Hawes to Reynal & Hitchcock. An eye for an eye and a tochus for a tochus, as Jezebel would say.

The theatre season has suddenly come alive with the arrival of some smash hits, notably Moss Hart's WINGED VICTORY (already published by Random House) and John Van Druten's THE VOICE OF THE TURTLE (about to be published by Random House). There are only three people in the cast of the latter play—Margaret Sullavan, Audrey Christie and Elliott Nugent, but the play is so wonderful that I didn't even mind sitting right next to your blankety blank mother-in-law. Right behind us was Noel Coward, arrived in town that very afternoon. Another smash hit is Carmen Jones, making two in a row for Oscar Hammerstein.

There is not much else to tell you except that we received a reasonably nauseating letter from Oppenbopper from India yesterday (he really seems to be having a wonderful time; practically no work to do as yet) and that Warren Marks dropped dead last week. Emily Hahn is back from Japan smoking great big black cigars for the photographers and stinking up the joint in general. Simon & Schuster are going nuts because Al Leventhal, Jack Goodman and Tom Bevans got their draft notices within the space of three days. Most of S & S's big books, incidentally, were delayed so badly in manufacture that they are coming out in a bunch about December 15th. I'm bleeding for them.

. . .

Write as often as you can. We love to hear from you. After everybody has read your letters, Jezebel takes them home to put under her pillow. A Happy New Year to you and I still think you will be back at that old desk of yours about a year from today. Nothing in the whole world would make me happier.

As ever,
Bennett

December 23, 1943.
CAPTAIN DONALD S. KLOPFER

WOULD GIVE YEARS PROFITS WELL HALF OF THEM ANYWAY TO HAVE YOU WITH US TODAY
LOVE

BENNETT

December 31, 1943

Dear Klopf:

This last letter to be dictated by the great Cerf to his inefficient and squirmy secretary is dedicated to the hope that you will have an exciting and happy New Year, which will end at the

desk where you God damn belong and are God damn well
needed.

The close of the year finds us in almost unbelievable financial
shape, with a present cash balance of over 190 you know what
in the bank, and 345 more in tax warrants. It is hard to remember that three years ago we were on our knees to those flint-
hearted so and sos across the street for dough to tide us over the
manufacturing season! Our total sales for the year will be close
to the two and a half million mark and the net profit for the last
six months, before taxes, not far from 400. Another million and
I promised Jez a $2.00 raise, although what with all the dough
she is making on the side picking up sailors on Broadway,
money now means very little to her and I have to use other in-
ducements. Why any woman should want more than two sable
coats is something I can't understand. . . .

I take it from the newspapers that you are in the very thick of
things and having the time of your fool young life, although I
realize that it is impossible for you to tell us any of the details.
Write as often and as much as you can, however, because every
word that you say echoes and re-echoes down the golden
canyons of 57th and 62nd Streets. My deep and lasting love to
you.

As ever,
Bennett

1944

Dear Don:

I have just received your letter of December 26th [letter missing] and it is plenty exciting to know that you are in the very thick of things. This afternoon we had a visit from a very attractive lady named O'Brien who told us that her husband trained with you out at Santa Ana. We shook hands over the mutual hope that both of you would soon be back here again.

The new paper order has come through and there's hell to pay about it. Not only is there an additional 15% cut, bringing the quota to 75% of the 1942 figure, but the order goes to incredible lengths to stop the device, commonly practised last year, of buying other publishers' unused quotas. There will be no more of that in 1944. What it will do to Pocket Books and other firms—not to mention ours—is rather painful to contemplate. The whole situation is so confused that it gripes me more than ever that you are not here to cope with it. Damn it, Klopfer, next time you stay home and let your grandchildren do the fighting! We'll have to cut down our activities to a considerable extent, of course, but from an actual matter of dollars and cents it won't make a very terrible difference—just a little less taxes to pay. Viking is going to take it on the chin because of this new order since they have a really good Spring list coming up. It grieves me to say that I think the new Fowler book on Barrymore is going to be a big best seller. We certainly got the rotten end of the stick from this such and such! Ah, well, our own list looks big too—so big, in fact, that I believe that if we went all out to put it over we wouldn't have a sheet of paper left over for the whole Fall season. Meanwhile, we'll be quietly mending our fences in the way of replacing worn-out plates for the Modern Library and getting going on some more whopping big Lifetime projects.

There isn't much social news aside from the fact that Joan Phelps is in Reno getting a divorce from Larry LeSeure so that she can marry Willy Wiseman, and that young Philip Langner, the 17-year-old son of Lawrence and Armina, is deeply in love. The girl's name is Betty Breslauer.

Take care of yourself, Schloppo, and remember that Jez and I both love you in our distinctive fashions.

As ever,
Bennett

JANUARY 11, 1944

MAJOR DONALD KLOPFER 0-906841

SALES CONFERENCE HALTED TO CHEER YOUR PRO-MOTION
        GREAT NEWS   LOVE

BENNETT CERF

January 11, 1944

Dear Klops:

All I seem to do these days is either to write or cable you congratulations for something or other, and I am getting pretty darn
sick of it. Anyhow, I think it is wonderful that you're a Major and
not quite so wonderful that you are approaching your 41st birthday (or even worse, your 42nd. Which is it?). Anyhow, you ven-
erable old codger, I hope you will enjoy a ripe old age which will
begin any minute now. Please write and tell us how it feels to be
an antique. We all wish we could see you with your gold leaf on
either shoulder but take it for granted that you look simply ele-
gant. See that you're a General by the time you come home.

You'll be interested in hearing the comment that was made by
one such and such when he heard that Georgie was in India.
"How nice for him," it ran. "When the war is over he will be
able to wear those campaign ribbons in his hair." Also, there is
a story of the private who had a beautiful girl out to dinner at
"21." She staggered him by ordering champagne cocktails,
caviar and a sirloin steak. "Hey," said the outraged private.
"Does your mother feed you this way too?" "No, she doesn't,"
conceded the girl. "But on the other hand, she doesn't expect
to lay me tonight either." I hope this gets by the censor.

Otherwise everything is quiet, Bob Haas leaves tomorrow for a
vacation in the South, and now that you both are away, Jezebel
and I will at last have the opportunity to fulfill an ambition she
has cherished for the past 25 years. We love you very much,
Major Klopfer.

As ever,
Bennett

Jan. 12, 1944

Dear Bennett:

Many thanks for your letter of December 31st. Your inefficient and squirmy secretary can type a mean Vmail letter. If you
want to get rid of her I suggest you send her over to me. I could
use a good secretary and typist in our department. She could replace about four GI's. And the CO says he can find no regula-
tion against having women in our Nissen huts, but he can find
no women, also.

The figures that you quote are too good to be true. Will we
be able to keep any of our profit at all? Wouldn't this be a good
time to start a helluva college text book department with the
gov't paying practically the whole bill and ready to really operate when the colleges go back to normal in a couple of years.
Fred Crofts is getting too old to stay in business. We can show
him figures to match his now. I really am anxious to see the
Spring list. Let this be an official request for the books on it before I get the list itself to request specific titles. Or can't you
send them to Jamie Hamilton for me? Are you resetting any of
the ML's and are we building up Lifetime books in these times
when anyone can sell books? I've got to have something to
come back to, Cerfie, the army as a career for me would be too
horrible for words even in my exalted new rank. I've been able
to borrow only one set of insignia so I'm not in good shape yet!

The work over here is grand when the weather doesn't keep
the boys from flying. We really work like the devil and have a
real responsibility in directing them to the target and out as
safely as possible. Evasion and escape, gunners aircraft recognition and all that sort of thing are the responsibility of my department and believe me, when men's lives are at stake you're
willing to work with them a great deal harder than for any other
reason. Our outfit is carving out a good record for itself. It's by
far the best of the new groups that have come over, and you can

follow its fortunes via Jimmy Stewart* every now and then. He's doing a good job and gets thinner and thinner all the time. It hardly seems possible, but it's true.

Our ration of liquor on the Base is one fifth of scotch for every five officers per month, so there's no chance of any dissipation from that angle. There are no towns near us worthy of the name and London is 3½ hours away so there's no chance of getting into trouble with any gals. I'm sick to death of this non social existence but I see no change except a few days in London later in the month. And those I'll take because I'm getting stale—I'd like to see Plummer and Hamilton, hear some talk other than airplanes and see if there's any civilization left in this here world.

The Russians are evidently doing a superb job. I hope to hell they romp thru' to the Channel. We'll probably be getting set for invasion when they hit the German border! There's been big shake up in command around here but that doesn't extend down as low as a Group. All we have to do is get the planes in the air and have them flown over the target!

All of which is very boring to you, I'm sure. I'm well and happy and lonesome as hell, but you can't complain about that when you're not risking your neck. Give my love to Thrup, and Saxe, and, of course, Bob and Merle, and Pauline, Lew & the gang. I can't write each one letters because I haven't the time or energy. Keep well, and I hope I'm back in my seat at 20 East damned soon. I do miss it.

Love,
Donald

*The movie star was a squadron commander in the 445th.

Jan. 22, 1944

Dear Cerfie:

So we've been cut to 75% of the 1942 paper tonage. Oh boy, is that going to raise hell with our volume. Have they cut newspapers and magazines that drastically and can we get any special allowances on stuff sold to Army and Navy? Am I glad that I have nothing but simple problems like trying to help these idiotic pilots not to get killed—and working out missions all night long only to have them scrubbed as they are warming up the engines! As I wrote Bob yesterday, I saw Jamie and Dick and John Strachey in London. Jamie hasn't a damned thing to offer. Dick's fine and John gave me the typescript of his novel which I haven't read yet. Celia is conscious of owing us $400 which she wanted to pay me but can't send until after the war. I told her to wait and send it when she could.

I feel mighty old, Cerfie, 42 to-morrow. We're no longer the young publishers of 15 years ago. God damn it—we have to keep our ideas young and keep up to the minute. This association with combat crews is good for me. But they are so unconcerned with what's happening in the world! My love to Thrup & Chris and all the gang. I sure miss you!

Love,
Donald

Feb. 8–44

Dearest Cerfie!

Here am I, listening to some lovely music coming over the radio from Calais I, a fine German propaganda station, having finally gotten a few minutes to myself to write to you. My CO is a gregarious fellow who can't stand being alone and happens to like to work all the time! The net result is that it's almost impossible for me to get any time to myself at reasonable hours. Beside which we've run nine missions in the last ten days as you've undoubtedly read in the papers. That's quite a strain on the department and the boss in particular! I didn't get to bed at all last night or two nights ago. But I'd a helluva lot rather have it that way than mope around the place with nothing to do. I'll certainly know the geography of Germany and France when this phase of the war is over if I don't get anything else out of it. But we really have been going a great pace—briefings around 4-30 in the morning—interrogations reports—teaching, studying and being assistant chaplains to the Combat Crews. It's a full time job. But I'm glad I'm here—much as I wish that I was home. Sounds silly but that's the way I feel. I guess I'm kidding myself but my department got the only Excellent rating in the big General's Inspection of a week ago, so I guess my job is being adequately handled. Anyway I have a lot of good boys working for me.

John Strachey recommended that I read "The New Economy" by Robert Boothby an interesting little book. I am enclosing herewith a self explanatory letter. Why not contact the guy. Harry Scherman would whirl in his golden seat if we published it. The only real objection is that it's too British in its treatment of the problem—but there 'tis. As I wrote you before, Jamie has nothing coming up originating over here and Chatto is doing practically no publishing. I got a nice letter from Sarah Ball the other day. She said Mannie said we might be out of stock of 100 MLs in the near future—what goes on? I haven't even received the Spring list yet. I know you've mailed it but it's not here and for the first time I feel really out of touch with Random House. Jesus, I'll have to learn the whole list over again, when, as, and if I get back.

I hear New York is gay and mad. People are spending money like drunken sailors and it's 1929 all over again only more so.

That's really a little depressing. How are Chris and Phyllis—when are you going to have another baby—are Saxe and Lew and the old gang happy? Is Pauline more beautiful than ever—how much do I owe Random House now—what is Red Lewis planning for a new book—did Walter Clark ever come in? Oh there are a million questions I'd like to ask. Don't bother answering them. And let me know that you and Bob are happy—and that you're having a good time out of life. I wish I were with you.

Love,
Donald

February 11, 1944

Dear Maje:

Haas looked so disgustingly healthy when he blew in from Florida that Miller, Commins, and Mr. and Mrs. Cerf turned right around and wrangled accommodations on a train headed for Miami next Thursday. I understand it is terribly overcrowded down there and filled with the worst gorillas in the country, but the thought of that hot sun and my tochus on a beach kind of balances everything. Seriously, we all need a couple of days of relaxation of that sort, because the going around here has been pretty hectic for a long, long time.

We are really seriously talking with Bob Linscott about having him come down to Random House. I am sure that if a deal can be worked out, you will be in favor of it, because I know that you share my feeling for Bob. He is no longer happy at Houghton Mifflin and, if he comes here, he will be able to take a terrific burden off my shoulders, particularly in regard to the entertainment and coddling of authors. I will let you know the minute something is settled. What held me back from talking seriously this long was the thought of post-war problems but, from the present look of things, there will be plenty of work for all of us, including Bob if he comes, for many years to come.

I have spent a lot of time with Dick Tregaskis. He is almost entirely recovered from his wounds and is pounding out a new book as fast as he knows how that will be bigger than GUADALCANAL DIARY. It is going to be called INVASION DIARY and will cover the raid over Rome (in which he participated), Sicily, Salerno and the whole battle of Italy up to the day on which he was hit. Then there will be several chapters on base hospitals and hospital ships—all first-hand, brand new stuff—and a final chapter comparing the Nazi and Jap fighting machines. After all, Dick is the first reporter who has seen both of them at first hand. I am terribly excited about the book.

Another great possibility is a book we are getting chapter by chapter from a guy down in Buenos Aires. The tentative title is ARGENTINE DIARY. If it comes off, it will be a bombshell. Add these two books to an already strong Spring list, and you can see that our only problem is going to be one of paper. Quent's book is an "A" book with the Book-of-the-Month Club, but I don't think it will be taken. Anyhow, it is a cinch that it will sell 50,000. Quent's doing a weekly radio program now and is more popular than ever. The [Edgar] Snow manuscript is not yet ready which is a break for us, since we couldn't handle it in the proper way at the same time as the Reynolds. . . .

You and your bunch seem to be doing a wonderful job. Keep it up and know that all of us think about you and talk about you constantly. I feel that this letter hasn't got much bounce in it, but I am simply pooped and know that you will take the will for the deed. Everything is in great shape here.

My love,
Bennett

February 21, 1944

Dear Don:

We were happy to get your cable about the Illustrated Modern Library. The books went like hotcakes and it burns us up to discontinue them for the time being. The paper situation being what it is, however, we have absolutely no choice in the matter. We are trying to work out some kind of a deal whereby A. S. Barnes & Co. can publish these Illustrated Modern Library books for the duration with all rights reverting to us again immediately upon termination of the war emergency measures. Whether Washington will approve of this or not we have no way of knowing. I will keep you posted. Meanwhile, we are going ahead with the necessary art work and plate setting of the next ten titles anyhow so, no matter what happens, we will be in good shape to go into the thing with a bang as soon as the necessary paper is available.

As far as the regular Modern Library is concerned, we definitely will not ever be out of 100 titles at a time. We decided to do most of the skimping on the Giant series. These books, of course, eat up far too much of the available paper in proportion to the profit realized. We may have to cut our list of active Giants down to somewhere around 15 to 22 for the duration, but I think you will agree that this is preferable to letting too many of the little ones go out of stock. Of course we'll be careful to see that the best selling Giants are always available, although we may have to ration orders on them. As you can see from the above, this is getting to be a perplexing and irritating business in some respects. And you can thank your lucky stars that you are missing plenty of heartaches. It has gotten to the point where a set of knockout reviews sends a publisher into a near panic. Good God, he says, clapping his hands to his head, I am afraid we've got another best seller on our hands. Isn't it terrible? I am not really kidding about this at all. When you have just so much paper to meet all demands, most of the kick of putting over a new book disappears completely.

To answer the other questions propounded in your note of February 8th:

1. Phyllis and Christopher are wonderful. Phyllis is now the official chairman of her department at 99 Park, and has been written up in several newspapers. When that dame gets under way, I pity anybody who blocks her path. Talk about juggernauts. Your first wife was an amateur compared with my Phyllis! As for Christopher, he knows his whole alphabet and is rapidly reaching the "why Daddy?" stage. My patience, it will surprise you to know, is not limitless and I am afraid that I am not exactly the best father in the world. I am really crazy about the runt.

2. I doubt that we will have another baby. Phyllis got more of a scare about the Caesarian than I suspected at the time. I guess we'll have to wait for another Harriman weekend! (Meanwhile, Edith Young is four months on the way.)

3. Everybody around here is as happy as can be expected. Saxe, Lew, Phyllis and I are shoving off Thursday for a couple of weeks of sunshine in Miami. I understand conditions down

there are incredible, but they can't take the sun and the beach away from us. That is all we want. I originally dictated this paragraph to Jez to read that the question whether Bob Linscott came with us or not was still in abeyance. Well, it isn't in abeyance any longer. Bob just called up from Boston to say he is definitely coming with us, and I am happier about this than I can say. I hope you will agree with me that his acquisition is a tenstrike for Random House—not so much right now when we are restricted by lack of paper, etc., but for post-war expansion when we'll really have an editorial board, in my opinion, that is better than anyone else's in America. Bob will be particularly valuable in the business of entertaining authors, agents and editors. Women fall for him like a ton of bricks. I had him for dinner about ten days ago and the next morning Beatrice Kaufman and Peg Pulitzer called up separately to ask for his telephone number. And a certain young lady, who shall be nameless but who was once married to you, exclaimed upon hearing the news, "Goody, goody, now I can really walk out." I went to some pains to explain to all of these worthy creatures that we were not getting Linscott down to take care of them! Saxe is delighted about the news and the only one who has any reservations whatever is Harry Maule. I anticipate a wee bit of trouble in that direction insofar as agents are concerned, but Bob is such a tactful fellow that I am sure everything will be ironed out in due course. The salary arrangement is a straight $200.00 a week with a small percentage to be agreed upon later on books that he is directly responsible for. Sooner or later we are going to have to give some of our key people a small stock participation in the business. That sort of thing is in the wind now and I think we owe it to some of the fellows around the office. If you have time, I'd like your views on this subject. Nothing, of course, will be done until you get back, but we ought to be thinking about it now.

. . .

Incidentally, when Houghton heard that Bob was thinking of leaving them, they offered him a staggering increase and anything else he wanted on a silver platter. He said ruefully that if they had given him half as much voluntarily he never would have dreamed of leaving. Isn't it funny how our estimation of something goes soaring when somebody else wants it? For instance, I never really cared much about Jezebel's fanny until I caught you potching her.

4. Your fourth question, in case you may have forgotten it, reads "Is Pauline more beautiful than ever?" By Pauline I presume you mean Jezebel. If this is true, why the hell don't you say so? Jezebel is definitely more beautiful than ever and has now reached the super-dreadnought or Madeleine Boyd class. A nearsighted gentleman mistook her yesterday for Alice B. Toklas. . . .

5. Red Lewis is definitely planning another novel. He says he's got the title for it already but won't tell us what it is. He also says he thinks it will be his most popular subject since ARROWSMITH. He expects to start work on it in about two months. We may have it for publication in the Fall of 1945. He is in very good shape.

6. Quent Reynolds' THE CURTAIN RISES looks like a runaway. The first edition of 26,000 copies is already sold out and 10,000 more are on press. The official publication date is March 6th. This book, like all the others on our list, are going forth to you regularly and I only hope that a few of them will actually reach you. I am also sending two more Spring catalogues to you in separate envelopes. Let me know if they arrive.

7. Walter Clark's manuscript ran to some 1200 pages and needed cutting. He stayed at my house for three days last week and he and Saxe had some long sessions which I think will produce the necessary results. The book has some wonderful stuff in it but, frankly, I don't think it's as good as OX BOW. The best novels on our list this year are LIMIT OF DARKNESS by Howard Hunt and a book by Samuel Hopkins Adams called CANAL TOWN, which has really got the old zing in it. Then we've got Dick Tregaskis' INVASION DIARY coming up. It will be a big season for us. Bob Haas will investigate Robert Boothby's THE NEW ECONOMY immediately and will write you about it as soon as he has some details.

That's enough about business for a while. Interesting as all these activities are, I am sure I don't have to tell you that any one of us would happily swap places with you in a minute. You're doing a job that is helping, in its infinitesimal way, to end the war; we're just betting along in the old groove waiting for you guys to finish it for us. It is true that New Yorkers are throwing money around like crazy, but this isn't quite as awful as it sounds. There are so many things they can't buy that there is all the more left for flinging away in restaurants, theatres and night clubs. And wait until they see their March 15th tax reports! I had mine made up early so I could get paid before I left for Florida. Wow! Keep pitching, Klopfer, and know that we all miss you and love you.

As ever,
Bennett

March 3–44

Dear Bennett:

By golly, I was glad to get your letter of Feb. 21 to-day. Do you know that is the first letter I've received from you this year! I haven't received either the Spring list or any RH books except the Illustrated ML's that Pat sent me. I'm sure you've written many. I know you send books but they just haven't gotten to me. Business certainly must be annoying what with all these restrictions and an unlimited market. But I'll be damned if I can feel sorry for the life you're leading what with you, Thrup, Lew & Saxe going down to Florida. I've had exactly four days off since Oct. 15th and that means days net, as we work seven days a week over here. It's amazing how one gets out of the habit of weekends or even Sundays off. And since they are sending over Groups without the grandchildren, now we are having to supply offices and EM to these Groups. That cuts down personnel and makes the work even harder. It would really be a strain if there was something around here that one wanted to do, but as there are no attractions about I don't mind it. But that's enough grousing now—I am tired and stale as all hell but I guess I'll be that way until the end of the war.

It seems too bad that the Giants have to go out of stock but if you can keep the regular ML up and not use contracts etc for the Giants during this war period I guess we can revisit this after the war. I should think the object of the game at the present time is to publish books that will sell 5000 copies the first year and will still be selling 5000 copies 20 years from now. Try to find them!

I didn't know we were once more negotiating for the services of one Linscott. I can't tell you how happy I'll be to have him in the RH family. You wouldn't have made a happier choice in the editorial end and I know Bob will enjoy working with RH and all of us will be delighted to have him added to the business. The sex life of at least six girls around town ought to be more

satisfactory now that he's moved to N.Y. That's quite an organization you and RRH are building up at Random House. I
wonder about two things. (1) will there be any reason for me in
it at the end of all this horrible mess and will I be any asset to
the business (2) will Random House be any fun at all as a "big
business" instead of our very personal venture? Oh well, I can
worry about that when, as, and if I return. As far as stock interests for the key people in the business is concerned, I'm all for
it if some satisfactory method can be devised so that when and
if they quit their interest can be repurchased by the company.
I've never heard of a minority stockholder getting out of a privately owned corporation with anything but hard feelings all
around. And once you have stockholders you have to start paying dividends, watching salaries and in general acting like an
honest corporation instead of working on the basis of "It's OK
if it suits the three of us." It's not a simple procedure and you
have to go into it mighty carefully or everyone will be unhappy
at the result.

I'm sorry to hear that Walter Clark's novel is not as good as
Ox Bow. In my mind, he's potentially the best writer we have—
but that second novel has to be really good. Have Saxe give
him the works. News of Red Lewis is grand—that's sure future
profit.

Keep your hands off Pauline. Just because I turn my back for
a few minutes don't try to take advantage of the poor girl.

And don't be a God damned fool, Cerfie, to want to change
places with me or anyone else over here in this God forsaken
part of England! Thank your lucky stars every day that you're at
home with your wife, kid and business and leading a pretty
normal life with friends and relaxation and stimuli at your command. This show hasn't the slightest element of fun about it. It's
nothing but hard work—a degraded type of excitement and
tragedy every damned time the boys take to the air and that's
every day that the weather permits. The flow of new runs and

airplanes seems endless and as we lose some another batch of expendables comes walking in. Every time a fully equipped B24 crashes $390,000 is signed away by the CO and ten lives under the age of 30 are snuffed out. It isn't pretty and you're lucky not to have anything to do with it. I still think I'm doing exactly what I should be doing but no one can ever make me say I like it or that I prefer it in any way to my normal, dull routine life. The whole air show is approaching a climax and we'll just keep pouring it on as the weather clears up a bit and we can move. It's going to be costly but last week's bombing proved to me that the old Luftwaffe can never stop us from hitting any target in Germany that we really want to hit. That goes for Berlin too! London is being kicked around a bit now, but nothing serious and we get a very minor share of it every week.

And now I'm about written out—but give my love to Thrup and that infant prodigy of yours. Please thank Louise* for her thoughtful letter and love to Saxe, Lew, Pauline and all of my friends at RH.

Love,

Donald

March 11, 1944

Dear Benito:

Your letter of Feb. 11 arrived to-day. I have already received and answered one written subsequent to that date. So you see how irregular the mail service really is.

Our December figures certainly were lousy in comparison with last year's! But the thing that I don't like to see is those old

*Louise Bonnino, RH juvenile editor.

inventory figures going down. I hope we are not just selling our birthright every time we make a good sale. God damn it this is the time to build for after the war when we will need it. I expect to be flat broke at the end of it because I'll probably have to sell what stocks I have to pay any income tax when I finally get out. I'll owe for '42, '43, '44 and '45 and I won't have the dough— Maybe I'll go down and live on the farm and vegetate. You fellows are doing a grand job without me there and I don't know whether there'll be any place when I return. The addition of Bob will take a lot off your shoulders. Lew certainly can handle the sales end—Bob Haas and Ray the manufacturing with time to spare for the general office work, and hell, that's all you really need. With Linscott to take some of the author work off your minds you will have time to look into other ends of the business that are top heavy with executives. Do you really think we can hold to that $2000000 level after the war? It seems fantastic to me but I suppose it's perfectly possible. I guess I always was a small time operator. And is it any fun anymore, or are you just developing a big audience like Doubleday's or S & S? We've had so damned much fun out of the business that I hate to think I'm a stranger to this new phase of it.

The 8th AF really went to town in the last couple of weeks. Give us two more of clear weather and we'll have the Luftwaffe in the ropes. Our boys have done a beautiful job! I don't imagine there'll be much rest between now and the end of the invasion, when, as, and if!

My best to all the people around the office—

Love,
Donald

March 21, 1944

Dear Don:

All of the wanderers are back home: Thrup, Saxe, Lew and my-self. We had a wonderful rest and arranged matters so that we were able to arrive in New York in the midst of a swirling snow-storm. Now we are ready for work on a major scale. It was a fine feeling to walk in and find Linscott toiling away for Random House. Getting him is, in my opinion, the smartest move we have made in a long, long time.

Two letters from you arrived the same day that I did. One of them was dated March 3rd and the other one March 11th. I note in both of them that you are concerned about (1) the general future of Random House, and (2) your own part in the pro-ceedings. I hasten to assure you that both worries could not possibly be more groundless.

Let's take up the future of Random House first. It is possible, as you suggest, that we may not be able to keep up a yearly pace of two million dollars or more, although I should say, offhand, that the odds are about five to one that we will. Here are my reasons:

1. Modern Library sales are growing so fast that I don't feel that the restoration of peacetime conditions can do more than temporarily interrupt the trend. The hundreds of thousands of Modern Library books that have been distributed through Army and Navy channels have introduced the series to God knows how many millions of new readers. If only one half of one percent of these boys retain an interest in books in gen-eral and the Modern Library in particular, our potential mar-ket will have multiplied about five times over pre-war standards. This isn't just dreaming; it is hard, cold facts. We

are taking advantage of present circumstances to make new plates for dozens of old titles, to replace bad translations with good new ones and, in general, to get the line in such shape that the minute paper restrictions and labor difficulties are things of the past we'll be in a position to go ahead with all stops pulled.

2. The reception of the Illustrated Modern Library books is nothing less than ecstatic. We are getting the art work and plates done on ten more titles at this very moment. We may not be able to print them until the war is over, but when we do get them out, we'll have a substantial nucleus for a new line with infinite possibilities.

3. The Lifetime Library has been receiving an increasing amount of our attention and Linscott's coming will intensify our drive in that direction. The Aquinas, as you know, is almost ready. Advance interest in it is enormous. We've almost finished setting the Wheatley Pepys in a two-volume set identical with the Plato. A one volume of St. Augustine is under way. Last night I got what I think is another thoroughly sound idea for the series, and that is a complete and unexpurgated Burton's ARABIAN NIGHTS. This has never been available in anything but an expensive ten or eleven volume set. I think we can boil it down into our two standard volumes and, if that fails, certainly into three. We will get the plates all made and have another item ready for post-war promotion that will bring an income, I feel sure, for the rest of our natural lives.

4. The flat juvenile market has only been tapped. Lew Miller has done a wonderful job of lining up toy accounts, many of whom have vowed to keep on with the line after the war is

over. There is no reason on earth why they shouldn't. The flat juveniles alone should support us in our old age—unless, of course, you feel you have to give Jezebel a new ermine coat every year.

5. To add to our flat juveniles, we've got plans afoot for a new 25¢ line which may work wonders. The notion is to translate Harper's phenomenally successful Tall Mother Goose into the 25¢ line. We are trying to work out a list of ten titles and are wavering between the name of Lofties and Tip Toe Books. This is all very hush hush and we are trying to guard the secret most zealously. If Duplaix ever dares to holler that we swiped an idea of his, we have only to remind him that when we complained about his duplicating our 50¢ and $1.00 titles in his 25¢ Golden Books, he said very vehemently that different priced lines in no way could possibly compete with one another. I really don't think there will be the slightest trouble along this line. Judging by the way the $1.00 Tall Mother Goose has sold, this format at a quarter could really be a gold mine.

6. To the already formidable stable of first-class writers that are now under contract to Random House, we can expect an addition of still more through the coming of Bob Linscott. We made it very clear to him that we don't want him to take any authors from the Houghton Mifflin list, but inevitably a couple of them will come with him. Carson McCullers, for instance, has already sworn that she will give a book to nobody but Bob. Furthermore, as you know, he has ins with people like Bernice Baumgarten that none of us could get in twenty years. This is all future stuff, of course, because we haven't got paper to take on any new people now—but it's the future years that we are talking about!

7. All kinds of new avenues of distribution for books are pending. Independent news dealers throughout the country have had such phenomenal success with Pocket Books that they are dying to get into higher price brackets. We've already made a few contacts that may prove invaluable later on.

8. We have just signed all the necessary papers for the launching of Random House of Canada. It is my hunch that this new setup will multiply the business that Macmillan was able to do for us up there ten times over.

I hope that all the above will satisfy you as to the future possibilities of our business. The beautiful part about it all is that the setup can remain a simple one, right under our own control, and with no possibility, in my opinion, of ever developing into a sprawling and unmanageable menagerie like the Doubleday outfit. You know that I share your abhorrence for impersonal "big business." I don't think Random House will ever get into that category.

Now let's get on to the part that you play in all of this. I honestly don't think that a worry of this sort would possibly have entered that fool head of yours if you hadn't been mentally upset by your long absence from everything you love best and the unholy strain imposed upon you by your present activities. You are part of the very fibre and bloodstream of Random House, you blithering idiot, and the fact that you are not here now hasn't altered that fact in the slightest degree. I assure you that not one day goes by but what at least three people groan "things will be different when that bastard Klopfer gets back here." Everybody has been doing the best that they can, but the strain has told on all of us and the day you come back you will find more stuff dumped into your lap than you can possibly handle. You may consider this an ironclad promise. If you will stop to reason coldly and calmly for a minute, you will see for yourself that if even half of the above plans come to fruition, the amount of planning, management and development will be simply enormous. Bob Haas has done a superb job with the manufacturing under most difficult circumstances, but I think he will tell you himself that the happiest day of his life will be when he can wrap the whole manufacturing problem in pink ribbon, tie a bunny on top, and throw it back to you.

I could go on in this fashion for ten more pages, but I hope that by this time even you will begin to realize how unutterably ridiculous your worries on this score have been.

As far as our immediate problems are concerned, you will have to get used to the idea of our inventory figures slipping downward. In the first place, every day finds more binding restrictions being placed on the amount of inventory that any firm is allowed to carry. In the second place, books go flying out on the day that they arrive from the bindery, so that it would be almost impossible to maintain any decent sort of inventory even if we were allowed to. We could very easily use our entire year's allotment of paper on Modern Library alone without printing one single Random House book. That will give you some notion of what we are up against. Fortunately, every other publisher in the country finds himself in precisely the same situation and not even the most unreasonable bookseller in the country (Mr. Kroch, for instance) dreams of grousing any more. They take what we give them and actually say thank you.

One last thing. You talk about being flat broke at the end of the war. My dear Klopfer, that is just a laugh. Despite the taxes and high costs and all kinds of other worries, this business has gotten into such shape that it is virtually impregnable. If you haven't got a nickel in the world outside of your share in Random House when the war is over, you will still be a very, very rich man. Furthermore, the rise in stock and bond values—which I believe will continue, with occasional interruptions—means that your mother's bankroll, Sam Goldsmith's bankroll, and most important of all to you, Pat's holdings, have increased enormously in value. In short, as the managing editor said to the escaped murderer when he had him sealed in a roll-top desk in THE FRONT PAGE, you're sitting pretty.

I am asking the notoriously undependable Jezebel to make three carbon copies of this letter. The four letters will be mailed at intervals of two days, so that one of them is almost certain to reach you. I simply cannot understand what's happened to all the other letters, books and catalogues that we have sent you. I am also sending you four Spring lists in separate envelopes. One of them *must* reach you. As for books, we will simply have to go on sending them and pray that an occasional one will reach you. Anyhow, think of what fun you'll have when you come home seeing a hundred or so Random House books you never set eyes on before. (Silver lining department!)

With my deepest love,

As ever,
Bennett

April 1, 1944

Dear Bennett—

April Fool's Day and I'm listening to the German propaganda broadcast from Calais I, Nuremberg etc. They have by far the best musical programs on the air around here so everyone listens. This was no fool's day for us.

COPY CENSORED FROM LETTER BY TAPE

That's the first bad day we've had since Feb. 24th so I don't suppose there's much to complain of. But I hate to be shooting craps with these boys on one night and have them disappear the next day.

I keep the situation map of the Russian campaign in my own office and the gains of the past week have been fantastic. They are doing such a beautiful job. I only hope they force our hand into doing a first class one ourselves. I wonder where the Germans will be able to make a real stand. They've done a bit of expert withdrawing themselves, if the "captured" figures mean anything. When invasion does come I imagine we'll be running two missions a day instead of our one a day program now. That will keep up the averages for Gen. Doolittle and will manage to keep us busy too!

I suppose by this time Linscott has fitted into the picture so damned well that it's as tho' he'd been there a lifetime. I'm really happy about Bob being there and I know that he'll do a real job for us with the sort of book that we're interested in publishing. When I saw Harold in London last month he was whining about the possibility of the Fowler book running away. He said publishers really didn't want best sellers now. What a predicament.

Love,
Donald

April 13–44

Dear Bennett:

An exciting day around here—our first original crew finished its tour of duty to-day—30 missions in four months of operation and they're now off combat status. They came back from Munich this afternoon and we were in the tower to sweat them out. They broke away from the formations and buzzed the tower—and I mean within ten feet of it in that big, clumsy plane shooting all the flares that were left in the plane, red, green, yellow, white—we fired rockets, flares, the big cannon and everything else around the place. The CO then brought the crew up here, gave them drinks and gave them all the DFC. Everybody was mighty happy—it could be done, altho' we have mighty few of our original outfit left to do it. Thirty missions in the big leagues is pretty hard to accomplish because the Germans still have plenty left. We lost two to-day, five yesterday and if it had been this crew I think our morale would have been shot to hell. As it is we forget the losses and point to the one who got thru' safely.

Last night we had R.H. Mottsan, remember the Spanish Farm Trilogy, up here with a lady psychiatrist, a school master and yours truly for an informal quiz program. One for the enlisted men and later in the evening for the officers. The audience asked any questions and we tried to answer. It was good fun and I must admit I was not too sharp as I hadn't been to bed at all the night before—briefed once at 5 AM and had the target changed so that I rebriefed at 830 for a ten o'clock takeoff. That was really rough but we got away with it. So you see time does not hang too heavy on our heads over here. I think the pace will be accelerated still further in the near future, altho' we have gone daily for the past six days.

Your long letter of March 21st was a joy to receive. I got all four copies of that letter in the same mail so you can see how regular everything is. I'm really not concerned in the future of

Random House as a money making institution. I am a little concerned in it as a publishing house as you and I think of a publishing house. I have such a horror of the Doubleday type of thing that our volume really scares me a little. We don't want to be Simon and Schuster's! I hope to Christ you're right about the extended ML market after the war and I think that making plates for the ML and Illustrateds is just about the best thing that we can do. The Lifetime is a dream and the more we can extend that the better off we are. Please send me the Aquinas when ready using this letter as a direct request which will enable you to send it to me without question. I have gotten the Reynolds and Mary Fisher and the four illustrateds that Pat mailed to me. In all things I think that Linscott will be a great asset to the firm. He knows a *good* book when he reads one, and don't you bully him with the crap that you let yourself in for, such as "Four Whores in a Brothel" or whatever that one is. The Burton is a sound idea—and the 25¢ juveniles are really a contribution—that's a sound idea. But don't count on those toy boys too much. They like novelties and books do not have the novelty appeal. Present enthusiasm won't last when gadgets can be made again. Please don't let the damned thing get so big that we can't run it ourselves and get some fun out of it and still think we're contributing a little something to the future of America. Sounds mighty pompous, but I like to kid myself that we can contribute something if we're intelligent about it.

Thanks for your kind words about the place I'll occupy. Remember these when I return. I hope you're right, but I'm not so damned sure that Ray can't do as good a job—by this time he ought to be good or you ought to have fired him. When I was last there I didn't know which would happen! I hope you're right about R.H. being in excellent shape from now on. It's hard to figure from the statements because I never know what is owed in income tax and I guess that's the most important single item now. Your remarks about the market as well as R.H. futures have a sound faintly reminiscent of 1929, altho' I think you're right. Of one thing I am reasonably sure. R.H. had better be a gold mine because I doubt if I'll have anything outside of that!

Heard from Marion that she's finally decided to split with Harry. I think that makes sense—what the hell, if she didn't have any fun with him why go on. Eight years seems to be about her limit. Damn, I'm afraid that gal is doomed to perpetual unhappiness. And I hear that my daughter is really beginning to grow up. It's hard to believe that she's evidently going to a French camp in Vermont this summer. I suppose Chris is jabbering away at a great rate now and probably is completely captivating. Wait until he gets some brains—they're wonderful then.

Come Christmas, Cerf, and you can cable me our bet about my being back at R.H. Unless this invasion hurries up and is more successful than we can hope for I'm not even sure that the European war will be over this year. I'll be in the ETO six months in three days. It seems like a lifetime.

Give my love to both Bobs and Saxe, Lew, Pauline, Louise and all the people I'd like to be with right now. Here's hoping that all you say is true and that I'm just a damned pessimist! I do appreciate your letter and all that it implies. You know full well how very much you mean to me. I haven't many *close* friends!

Love,
Donald

April 14, 1944

Dear Donald:

Your letter of April 1st arrived with a great big hole cut out of the middle. This is the first letter of yours to this office that has ever been censored. I guess you got a little bit too explicit about what was going on in your neck of the woods, but you and the censors may be assured that all of us here have very good imaginations.

Good news continues to be available in bunches as far as Random House is concerned. In the first place, Washington has approved our transferring of the Illustrated Modern Library in toto to the A. S. Barnes Company for the duration. We'll get a royalty on every copy they sell and, furthermore, we'll get the whole thing handed right back to us as soon as the war is over. Aside from the royalty that we'll get, which will amount this year to somewhere in the neighborhood of $20,000.00, this means that we will be able to cash in immediately on the wonderful reception the first books got and not have too long a lapse go by before the second lot is available. From the continuity point of view, this is most important. In the second place, Harry Scherman and Merry Wood were so delighted with the looks of the Illustrated Poe that they bought it for their next dividend. This means that we'll simply blow up the pictures and the text page and make a regular Random House trade book out of it for a couple of years before we shoot into the Modernlibe. I wouldn't be surprised if we made almost enough on this one dividend to pay the entire plate cost of the first five Illustrated Modernlibes. The rich get richer!

There may be one more stray piece of news next week. The People's Book Club, which has now grown to some 160,000 a month, is teetering on the brink of taking Samuel Hopkins

Adams' CANAL TOWN. Even without them, this book will have a 15,000 advance. If they do take it, I am afraid we've got another real best seller on our hands which will give Haas a few more sleepless nights!

As for general business, we are doing all we possibly can and more. The sudden decision not to draft men over 26 for a while gives Joe Aaron a respite but, of course, this whole thing may be upset overnight. The draft board issues a new set of rules about three times a week and everybody within draft age is living in a state of confusion and suspended animation.

Yesterday was Thrup's 29th birthday and we celebrated with dinner at "21" where at least ten people asked for you and sent you their love, including one very beautiful girl whose identity was a complete mystery to me—probably one of the 9000 dames that you collected in that sophomore year of yours, every detail of which makes me shudder.

We all miss you terribly and have got enough things piled up for you when you get back to keep you occupied 27-½ hours a day for your first nine years back at the office. One thing you had better steel yourself for, my boy: Jezebel's fanny is definitely not what it used to be. It simply can't take it any more.

Sorrowfully,
Bennett

May 1–44

Dear Bennett—

I'm sure I don't have to tell you that we have seen many a busy time of it and I haven't had either the energy or inspiration for much correspondence. We've been blessed with a kind of good weather which has enabled us to operate every day and two missions on some days. The boys are getting pretty well worn out, but they seem to be able to go just as well when they're a bit tired. May Day has come and gone with no invasion but I guess it can't be too far off now. I wish they'd start and succeed so we could get the hell out of here and on our way to the final phase of the whole thing. Your friend Jones, the silent one, just led a beautiful mission in which they kicked the s—— out of a target. What a pleasure! I guess it must be beautiful in town and down at the country now. I wish I could get out more but my hours are so impossible that I don't move off the base. Love to the gang & Thrup—and yourself—

Congrats on your Spanish statement.

Donald

May 7–44

Dear Bennett:

Just received your letter of April 14—together with Bob's of the 27th. I'm sorry you are now being pestered by the censor. I can't imagine what I wrote that could be censored but we're dependent on the digestion of the censor and that is that. . . .

We're in a continual grind now—missions every day that the weather possibly allows. We're all steamed up to run enough missions per day to support an invasion. I was down in London to a meeting this week and I went to theatre and dined with Lynn. He's doing a good job, I believe— Didn't have time to see any one else in London as I had some shopping to do plus not much time.

You're slipping, Cerf, to have a beautiful girl ask for me and not even find out her name. I could use a beautiful girl over here, yes, even two or three.

Life is not too exciting here right now. To us it's something of a lull altho' we are very busy.

My best love to all—and yourself, of course.

Donald

May 12—44

Dear Bennett—

This should reach you vaguely around your 46th birthday. We seem eternally fated to spend our birthdays apart, my lad— but I guess this time there's a good reason for it. Anyway you know that I wish you all the luck, good things and happiness in the world. I don't have to tell you that. I'm sorry I can't celebrate with you but I'll have a drink to you at the Officers Club Bar—you can buy me one when I get back!

Things around here are going along at a steady pace—the steady pace meaning working the ass off all of the combat crews—we ground personnel can take it all right but it's a terrific strain on the crews. Daily flying of long tough missions just can't be done—and that's what the boys are doing—But to-day they did some of the best bombing I've ever seen in a long penetration deep into the Third Reich. They really plastered a synthetic oil plant and I have the pictures to prove it! We take vertical photos of all bombing and it's amazing what the damned things show up.

Of course the only thing on every one's mind these days is "When will it start?" We're all set for it, have lots of new planes and are all set for a *really* grueling couple of weeks. I do wish that it may be successful as I want to get out of this theatre and home if possible—or if not home at least on to the next phase—China or India. Life is dull around here.

Had dinner with Lynn in London last week—he seems sort of fed up, too. Saw a terrible show with him. . . .

My very best love to Thrup—bounce Chris once on the big knee for me.

And again—Congratulations!

Love,
Donald

May 19, 1944

Dear Donald:

Your birthday letter arrived a whole week early and pleased me more than I can say. How the hell you can remember a birthday in the midst of what you are doing passes my understanding; if it weren't for that undependable creature called Jezebel I would never remember an anniversary or birthday from one end of the year to the other! I echo your sentiment that this may be the last of our natal days that we spend apart for a long, long time to come. I grant you that the odds are against our being together on January 23rd, but after that I cling to the hope that our chances are good!

. . .

I have finally completed the manuscript for the new Pocket Book of Anecdotes that I have been slaving over, and now I will be able to take it a little bit easier for a while. The Fall catalogue has gone to press and we'll have a number of weeks to devote exclusively to the Lifetime Library and the Modern Library. We are going over the latter series title by title, examining the plates, introductions, translations and all that sort of thing so that, by the end of this year, although we may be out of stock of a lot of titles temporarily, we'll be ready to shoot full strength as soon as conditions right themselves. On the Lifetime end, as I think I have already told you, we are ploughing ahead with the plate setting on a three-volume unabridged ARABIAN NIGHTS and the two-volume Wheatley Pepys. Bruce Rogers has designed a beautiful new title page for a Lifetime Gibbon for the text of which we will, of course, use our Modern Library plates.

The new titles for the Modern Library this Fall I think are fine. We have finally gotten permission to do the Commager-Nevins SHORT HISTORY OF THE UNITED STATES in the Modern Library. The book now ends with Pearl Harbor, but Commager is doing a new introduction for us bringing the story right up to the minute. For our second title, Edgar Snow is revising RED STAR OVER CHINA, bringing that one up to date too. The third title is TWO YEARS BEFORE THE MAST. You may recall that James D. Hart did an introduction for this project way back in 1936. This seemed a good time to carry it through because a big movie version of the tale will be released in the Spring. The fourth title is THE COMPLETE POETRY OF DOROTHY PARKER, which we finally wangled from Viking. Her Short Stories have been one of our best-selling titles this year. We are only doing one Giant because of paper difficulties, and that one is the THREE MURDER NOVELS that has gone so well in the Random House edition. (Do you remember the time Pop* bound up all 5000 copies of the first edition? How he'd chuckle if he could see the sales record today!)

The graft on subsidiary rights grows more and more staggering all the time. The Literary Guild is using THE CURTAIN RISES as one of four current bonus books. Their first print order is 100,000 copies! That means $6000.00 for our share without turning a hair. Milo Sutliff [at Doubleday] is certainly riding high these days. All of his clubs and promotions are coining money, and I daresay he had more than a little to do with the sudden resignation of Malcolm Johnson from the Doubleday outfit last week. That news came as a bombshell to the publishing world. Harry Maule's face was a study when he heard it. Nobody knows what Malcolm's future plans are going to be.

Linscott has already made himself a permanent part of the outfit here. He is busy lining up young authors for post-war operation, a task for which I believe he is better fitted than anybody else in the whole publishing business. I have also got him and Saxe tearing their hair out over a new American dictionary for Random House. We want to be sure we've got the right setup for this project and then, by God, we are going ahead with it come hell or high water.

In short, my dear Major, current books are taken care of and, as you can see from the above, we are now all devoting ourselves principally to the dream that we share with you: a firm, solid backlist that will support us, I hope, for the rest of our lives.

---

*Bennett's father worked for a time at RH in charge of stock. Books were sometimes printed but not all bound until needed.

. . .

Don't be a God damn fool and overdo it. Remember that there
are a few million other guys in the Army besides Donald S.
Klopfer!

My deep love to you.

As ever,
Bennett

June 3—44

Dear Bennett:

Just received your most heartening letter of the 19th— My
birthday letter must have really romped on to you. That's quite
some service, but you can see it's not as fast coming this
way. . . .

Had a vacation to-day, consisting of only one mission this
morning and an inspection by the General. He was most com-
plimentary about my section—it's the best in the Division—
and paid the final compliment of not even bringing his A2
along. Consequently we're the white haired boys these days
and will be unable to get the smile off our CO's face for at least
48 hours. I got a great kick out of the first heavy bombers
to land in Russia yesterday. I knew those bases were being
built but I didn't know when they'd get going. We are at
greater strength now than we were before and will have to keep
up a steady ground until it's over. But it certainly agrees with
me. I don't know if I'll ever get back to going to bed and sleep-
ing a whole night thru'—but I'd like to try it sometime in the
future.

I appreciated Thrup's letter very much. I love to hear good things often. Damn—I miss you & Pat. . . .

Give my best to Linscott. I know he's doing a superb job for R.H.— Love to Bob, Pauline, Saxe, Lew & all the gang—and a special bit for you!

Donald

June 21, 1944

Dear Klopf:

Your letter of June 10th [letter missing]—the first line to reach us from you since the invasion—arrived an hour ago and has already made the rounds of the entire office. We were sure that you were okay, but it was mighty good to see that illegible scrawl of yours anyhow.

It is harder than ever these days to concentrate on business, but everything is banging along almost automatically in wonderful shape. We have sold Chris Massie's THE LOVE LETTERS to Hal Wallis for his first production. (He used to be top man at Warner Brothers, but is now going in for himself. His pictures will be released through Paramount.) Wallis paid us $35,000 for the property, of which 20% is ours. Not bad for a guy whose two previous books failed to reach the 4000 mark! The new book is a rather queer one too and, before this sale, I wouldn't have bet a plug nickel it would go higher than THE GREEN CIRCLE. Now, however, there is no telling what we'll do with it.

Reader's Digest has bought a hunk of Dick Tregaskis' new book, INVASION DIARY. The book is a peach. It may be hurt, of course, by all the subsequent developments in the war. Last year we'd have sold 100,000 of it. Now we'll be very happy if we can get it up to the 30,000 mark.

In the next letter I hope to have some definite news for you about the organization of a staff to really get to work on our long-dreamed-of Random House Dictionary. If possible, I want to call it the Random House Concise American Dictionary, and have it more or less uniform in size and scope with the Oxford Concise Dictionary. The mere word that we were working on such a project brought inquiries from the Grolier Society (publishers of the Book of Knowledge) and the Britannica people, who would like to work out a deal with us of some sort or other. It is obvious that if we ever do get a good dictionary we'll make a modest fortune on it and, in my mind, this is now Project Number One on the Random House future possibilities chart.

Lewis Browne has delivered the final manuscript of THE WISDOM OF ISRAEL. It should be a 1945 leader and sell in a class with the Lin Yutang WISDOM OF CHINA AND INDIA. We are also scheduled to get Walter Clark's finished manuscript of Trembling Leaves next week, but I believe we'll hold it for 1945 too. We really are strapped for paper for the rest of this year.

The big laugh of the month is that I am now a Simon & Schuster author. Dick and Max read the manuscript of THE POCKET BOOK OF ANECDOTES that I turned in and informed me that if I would let them do it as a S & S book first, they thought they could sell 50,000 copies or more. Big hearted Cerf was very generous about it and told them to go ahead. The book will be called TRY AND STOP ME, and if I am not run out of town when it appears, I may have some fun out of the whole thing, not to mention quite a bit of dough. I would say that the average age of the stories in the book is 67½ years—

which, by sheerest coincidence, happens to be the age of the young lady who is typing this note. (Jezebel said that this would lead you to believe that I have a new secretary, but I assured her that that dumb you weren't.)

Our social life is pleasant but unexciting. I had lunch with Marion yesterday, prior to her departure for Reno. This seems to be getting to be a tradition with us, but she wasn't too pleased when I pointed the fact out to her. She is really in pretty good shape, all things considered, and, in fact, informed me (1) that she is changed, and (2) that she now has a sense of humor. Where did we hear these words before, Klopfer?

As Phyllis wrote you, your daughter Lois has suddenly become a rather stunning and self-possessed young lady. She is really a wonderful kid.

That's all, you hyena, except that I wish the hell you'd get finished with that piddling around in England and come home to do a little work. It's getting so that I have to come in mornings at 10:30.

My deep love,
Bennett

July 1–'44

Dear Bennett:

. . . Congratulations on becoming an S & S author. It lowers you in my opinion because you know what I think of them as "class" publishers—now you're in the same class as Trader

Horn . . . and the 200th Cross Word Puzzle Book. What are you going to do with all of your dough, or does Uncle Sam take care of that?

I was down in London this week for a meeting and had my couple of days and nights with the "doodle bug."* It's a trim little ship and the most important thing about it is that it makes a helluva racket and you can hear it for quite a ways. Then there's a couple of second's silence and a big bang. Either you're all right or you aint—and that's that. But between the invasion and the doodle bugs London is now nice and empty—I stopped at the Savoy without reservations—they almost seemed glad to see me!

The Russians say *they* will win the war in 90 days no matter what we do—the best opinion around here is about four months, so I guess we'll be packing to go to China in the fall. I'm getting mighty optimistic but it seems to me that the war is actually in its final phase and things are going extraordinarily well!

The pace has slackened a bit around here—we're back to some strategic bombing rather than tactical—and I'm getting fed up. You'd better train down to get in at 10 o'clock because I don't intend to do any work for a long time after I return. I'll be no asset to Random House.

My best to Bob, Saxe, Lew, Pauline and the gang.

I hear Thrup has gotten beautifully thin. I think that's great!

Love,
Donald

*The German V-2 Buzz Bomb.

July 12, 1944

Dear Klopf:

It's been so hot in New York for the past ten days that work has been virtually at a standstill, and the various Mrs. Klopfers certainly knew what they were up to when they dispersed to Nantucket, Reno, and God knows where else. (I never have been able to keep track of the Klopfer women.)

We will soon be in the midst of the presidential campaign. To the vast discomfiture of Mr. Robert K. Haas, a straw vote in Random House office last week resulted in fifty votes for F.D.R. and a complete zero for Dewey. The funniest crack about the latter was pulled by one of his own supporters, Alice Longworth. She said he looked exactly like the bridegroom on top of a wedding cake. The high spot of the Republican convention came when Clare Boothe Luce got up to make a very nauseating speech. She was dressed in a simple little white frock and the ribald delegates began hollering "Take it off, take it off." My own hunch is that the President will be re-elected in a landslide. In fact, I have given the aforementioned Mr. Haas four to one odds.

De Gaulle's visit to America resulted in the most spontaneous demonstration of enthusiasm that has been seen in these parts since Lindbergh came back from his original flight to Europe. I was invited to a reception for him and when he entered the room, I started pressing forward to see him at closer range. When I discovered that the lady next to me was Miss Marlene Dietrich, I started pressing in a different direction. A good time was had by all. The Little Flower was almost trampled in the rush. When the picture of him posing with De Gaulle came out the next day, it looked even funnier than Mutt and Jeff. Fiorello was caught with his tongue hanging out of his mouth—a ludicrous picture that reminded me of Wolcott Gibbs' old crack that the Mayor had the peculiar knack of always getting himself photographed between expressions.

There isn't much business news. Perelman's CRAZY LIKE A FOX has caught on like wildfire and will double his previous best sale. TALES OF TERROR has crossed the 20,000 mark and if we had the paper, I think we could sell 100,000 before the holidays. Ed Snow's new book is an "A" book at the B.O.M.C. and we have got our fingers crossed. At the worst the Guild has offered to take it as a dividend so the book is in under any circumstances. Incidentally, the B.O.M.C. has just selected J. Marquand as the fifth judge, rounding out that body for the first time since Heywood Broun died. (In case you didn't know, Fadiman replaced the late Bill White about a month ago.)

Dick Tregaskis is thoroughly recovered and will be leaving for England in a few days' time. I have told him a lot about you and he is anxious to meet you. Please drop him a line in care of: P.R.O., Supreme Allied Headquarters, London, and tell him how he can get in touch with you, either by phone or letter. I think he'll have sufficient credentials to be able to come and see you at your base if you can't get down to London. He is a wonderful guy and I know you'll like him. Besides that, he'll be able to give you all the latest dope on Random House and its merry minions (including Mignon Eberhart).

The only other breathtaking news I have for you at the moment is that after twenty-three years of married life, Leonard and

Helene Gans have busted up. The next thing you know, Charles Evans Hughes and his wife will go pfft!

Love and kisses, and come home soon. This is an order!

As ever,
Bennett

July 22, 1944

Dear Bennett:

I haven't written for quite a while—but that's merely because of a combination of being busy and very stuck on the Base with nothing to write about except operations—and I can't write about them! We've been going along at a good steady pace and have done some excellent bombing in the past week—any time the weather is good enough for our boys to get a good visual run on the target they can plaster it—the thing to find over here is the visibility! I'm managing to keep busy but I have plenty of help now and my job here is done. All is running smoothly—and there's a tendency to get bored as the very devil with the whole setup.

The war news really looks fine now. I don't know whether this attempt on Hitler's life is a phoney or is on the level but either way it's to our benefit. The Russians are still performing their miracles—the Italian line is moving—the beach head is, at least, secure and we'll bust out of that when we've piled enough stuff in there so that we can really drive ahead. Even the Japanese deal is looking up, and as long as we don't fall for a lot of tricky government changes the end is in sight. Then our troubles will really begin—settling the whole mess.

The final figures for R.H. certainly looked good—here's hoping we can do as well this year. I suppose with your colossal outside income R.H. is becoming chicken feed for you, but remember, you bastard, I'm dependent on it for eating! By the time I've paid my back income taxes I don't expect to have any dough outside of this business. I receive letters from everyone saying how well Thrup is looking these days and that Chris has become a fixture around the office. That's mighty fine. If they throw me out of the Army before the next campaign there's a chance that you'll win your bet yet. I certainly hope you do as I'll like nothing better than to get back to R.H. and home.

I haven't been off the Base in a month so no news. Give my love to all at the office—and yourself of course.

Donald

August 18, 1944

Dear Don:

This is to report that Private Cerf has returned to duty at 20 East 57th Street, bronzed, rested and shorn of all pot-belly by four to six sets of tennis a day and God knows how many swims. We managed to miss the greater part of the worst heat wave that has hit the Eastern part of the United States in fifty years. This doesn't mean that we didn't get our share up in Maine, where the temperature hit an unbelievable daily average for a week of 93 degrees, but at least there was no humidity up there and the lake was always nearby for quick relief. I really had a fine time, and Natalie only spent two hours of the three weeks talking about you and unfinished business of one sort or another that she sincerely hopes some day may be consummated.

Chris took to the place like a duck takes to water, and I really got to know him better than I ever have before. He will be three years old tomorrow and is really turning into a great kid. I am also very bullish on Jimmy Manges, who was with us on the vacation and is turning out to be a swell youngster in every respect.

When I got back I found everything at Random House in apple-pie order: business fine and the outlook for our Spring 1945 list remarkably good. We'll start off with the postponed Aquinas, Lewis Browne's anthology, THE WISDOM OF IS-RAEL (a perfectly swell job), Walter Clark's novel which is finally shaping up, and George Stewart's new book which has brought raves from authorities on the subject who have read the manuscript. That is a sound nucleus, my boy, and there will be plenty of money-making trimmings to surround it.

I would now like to touch on a subject that is very close to my heart. It seems to me, if I may say so, that you have done your full share for the U.S.A., and that it would be almost inexcusable for you not to take advantage of a discharge, if one is offered to you, when the European phase of the war is ended. It is no longer a case of all of us fighting for our lives. I think it is fair to say that our victory is now absolutely certain and that it is only a question of how long a time it will take to bring it about. Under the circumstances, I think that a guy of your age has done more than his share in giving two and a half years to the cause. You can let younger fellows finish up the job and can come back to all the things that mean the most to you, and know that you have well earned the right to enjoy the rest of your life. A lot of fellows you know of 38 to 40 who had commissions and were stuck in this country are getting out as fast as they can, or at least are trying their damndest to. . . . Please bear in mind that we really need you here at Random House. We've got all kinds of plans for the future and we simply won't be able to carry them off unless you are here to shoulder your part of the load. I am not kidding about this, Don. I simply don't think there are any two ways to look at it. I am very anxious to hear your reactions to this line of thinking. I can honestly tell you that I think the first day I see you back at your desk here will be the happiest of my entire life.

As ever,
Bennett

September 6, 1944

Dear Don:

No word from you in several days now, but I suppose you are so busy you haven't time to write. It certainly looks like the end for the Nazis, and Wall Street evidently concurred in this feeling today, because it staged one of its little old peacetime busts. Our old friend Dorothy Thompson is picking this moment to nauseate and disgust people by yapping for a soft peace at the very moment when I think we should be toughest. I think she's gone mashuga.

. . .

Under separate cover, I am mailing you a copy of a form letter that we are sending out to the entire book trade to put them au courant with the Modern Library situation. The very first thing that we will do when paper restrictions are lifted is to get the Modern Library back into stock 100%. As you know, we've re-made a lot of the plates and brought several of the anthologies up to date. Once we get the new numbers all into stock, it is going to be a better series than ever.

We've fallen into another potential JUNIOR MISS situation. Carl Randau and Leane Zugsmith's little novel, THE VISITOR, which we published several months ago, has been made into a play that will be produced by Herman Shumlin this Fall, and the Warner Brothers have already bought it for a minimum of $150,000.00. We're in for 10% of one half on all dramatic and picture rights. (The other half goes to the playwright who adapted the story.) In other words, we've finally struck gold in Leane, proving that with the world in its present condition, absolutely anything can happen.

I took Pat down to your safe deposit box yesterday and pulled out some deed to the Mt. Vernon property that your mother wanted. You evidently forgot to give Pat the power of attorney to this box before you left and, judging by her comments, you will be hearing something about this when you come back. I think you will be able to take it. The only other hot news I have for you at the moment is that a former wife of yours over the telephone yesterday called me a hypocrite and a heel. I expect her to do better when she really gets warmed up.

As soon as you have the faintest idea what the immediate future holds in store for you, please write as many details as you are allowed to. As the time grows obviously nearer for your return to

Random House, we are all getting more and more impatient. Jezebel, for instance, has sworn not to shave again until you come back. It's the Elliot Paul influence.

Love,
Bennett

Sept. 13–1944

Dear Bennett—

Back at the Base again—after a week of travel around the south of England. Saw Salisbury, Winchester, Oxford, Canterbury, Dover and London— Dover's like a ghost town and I found out why when I was there as the Germans sent over a salvo that sent me sassying for the train as fast as my long legs would carry me. That artillery is dangerous! Had lunch with John Strachey—saw Stephen Spender at his club—John's going to run for Parliament and continue to write—says he. . . .

I just received your two letters—Aug. 18 & Sept. 6—and I can assure you that as soon as this act of the show is over I'm going to make every effort to get out of the Army and back to R.H. Thanks for your kind words—but R.H. seems to be doing gloriously without me. These August shipments are really something! Bob writes me that you're thinking seriously of buying a leasehold on the 57th Lex Bldg. I should think that if real estate is having anything like the inflation that all else is having this would be a lousy time to do such a thing. Obviously without really knowing anything about it I can't express an opinion—but it sounds like a helluva chunk for us to write off. That overhead has a tendency to remain when business slackens off a bit.

I can't tell you how anxious I am to get out of the whole

thing now and get back to Pat, Lois and all of you. This is no longer any fun—I'm no good on the winning side—as soon as I know anything definite—I'll let you know. In haste.

Love,
Donald

Sept. 23–44

Dear Bennett—

Not much to write about these days. We had two missions in the last two days and were stood down again to-day. The weather seems to be Hitler's best friend these days. Outside of a flight over to France I haven't done a damned thing worth talking about and I didn't stay in France long enough to do anything. Or did I write you that in my last letter.

Am in the midst of Argentine Diary which I find a very interesting and frightening book. How in hell are we going to stop all of this damned nonsense? In prolonging the war I think Hitler is going to allow us to cure the Germans but the damned bug has spread to all corners of the earth. I won't feel that this war is won until Franco is thrown out of Spain, but Winston and FDR seem to think that he's all right. They don't need anything that he has anymore—why do they still pamper him? What I started out to do was thank you for the two books which did come thru' at long last. I'd begun to despair of getting any books thru' the mails altho' I knew you've sent them. The more I think of buying that leasehold at 57th Lex, the less I like the idea. I'd a helluva lot rather buy a small building that we could occupy in its entirety except for the store, than a big chunk like that which would put us in the real estate business. Or if we'd bought it when the N.Y. market was down that would be another story but I can't believe that prices aren't up if space is scarce. Obviously, however, whatever you and Bob decide is completely agreeable to me.

The war goes well but the supply problem is really tough and I suspect will continue to be until Boulogne, Calais and maybe even Antwerp are operating as ports. It's a long hand across France and we raised hell with those bridges for months. We can take in a lot by air but weather makes that unreliable. Here's hoping that the British can really turn the flank of the German defenses and make a sizeable dent into Germany.

Give my love to Thrup, Chris, Pauline and all my friends at the office. I hope it's not too long until I see you again.

Love,
Donald

September 27, 1944

MAJOR DONALD S KLOPFER 0-906841
BOOK OF MONTH CLUB AND WE HAVE SIGNED
AGREEMENT WITH GROSSET DUNLAP TO BUY
CONTROL LATTER IN SIXTY DAYS CLUBS SHARE
SEVENTY FIVE PERCENT OURS TWENTY FIVE PER-
CENT HARPERS WILL PROBABLY PARTICIPATE ALSO
WE WILL HAVE COMPLETE MANAGERIAL RESPONSI-
BILITY TOTAL INVOLVED SOMETHING OVER TWO
MILLION BELIEVE BEST THING THAT EVER HAP-
PENED TO US BUT MUCH EXTRA WORK HOPE YOU
CAN TAKE OVER SOON WRITING

BOB BENNETT

October 2, 1944

Dear Don:

I am dictating this letter to Jezebel in the dining room of 132 East at 9:15 P.M. on Friday, although I know she won't be able to type it for you and get it off until Monday. This is the very first moment I have had to write you the details of just about the most hectic week in the career of Random House. I have read the carbon copy of Bob's letter to you, so I know that by this time you have all the bare details at hand, but I know equally well that you will want to know some of the sidelights. I will try to hit the highlights for you in this letter.

The wonderful part of the deal is that we snatched it right out of the jaw of Marshall Field and of the smarty pants at Simon & Schuster at the very last minute. The maiden was just about to be burned at the stake when the U.S. Marines dashed into view. Marshall Field will go right on with his deal with Dick and Max and the ubiquitous Mr. Shimkin, but we put one hell of a crimp in his plans for the time being anyway. The general setup was a terror. Field was to buy Grosset (with Doc Lewis acting as his manager) and then was to buy a big hunk of Pocket Books, People's Book Club, Cuneo Press, and Simon & Schuster itself. Don't ask me why the hell Dick and Max want to sell part of their business. Personally, I think they are drunk with dreams of empire and are being led blindly by Shimkin, who may be getting just a little bit too smart for his own good. The deal with Sears Roebuck on the People's Book Club has been a pip. Their membership is close to a quarter of a million already. Also, through Max Schuster's becoming a director of the Encyclopedia Britannica they are all mixed up with the University of Chicago on some elaborate publishing plans that may turn out to be something like that list of esoteric tomes that Arthur Rubin submitted to us some years ago (remember?). Anyhow,

there they were with Field's millions, Shimkin's shrewdness—
and Sears Roebuck in the background with a new book concern, a Grosset reprint, the People's Book Club, and Pocket
Books, with Cuneo Press to print the stuff. What a package
offer they could make to any author. The whole publishing fra-
ternity was running around in near panic—with Donald Grosset the most scared of all.

Speedy work on the part of Harry Scherman and our own
Robert K. Haas saved the day. Bob really did a superb job on
the whole negotiations. By Monday morning, when the deal
was finally set, sheets of flame were spurting from both his nos-
trils and a near-sighted lady mistook him for the Twentieth
Century Limited. We gave Harper's twenty-four hours to decide whether they wanted to come along or not. If you can
imagine old Henry Hoyns making a decision of this importance
in twenty-four hours, you are a better man than I am. Cass Canfield, however, pulled his end of the deal off. . . .

So now we are all set. We've got sixty days to take over the
joint. Don Grosset will ride along, but of course we'll need
some stronger, tougher and more up-to-date management
above him. We've got to throw out a couple of hundred items
that don't carry their weight on the list any more. We've got to
re-jacket good properties that are still packaged in their 1905
format. We've got to replace a few old dodoes who should have
been put out in the old folks' home ten years ago. We've got to
get out and bid for some of the current best sellers that have
been going to Doubleday and Ben Zevin simply because nobody from Grosset was alert enough to go after them. Above
all, we've got to get started in the chain store and drugstore
field. Grosset has simply let this end of the business go by the
board—an unbelievable miscalculation because Doc Lewis
with his Triangle Books, and Zevin with his Tower Books have

shown, in two years, that this is where the great mass markets of the future are going to be really developed.

This brings me down to a little more talk about Mr. Ben Zevin. I don't remember whether you even met him or not. In the two years since you've been away from the book business, he has grown from a little peanut to a guy whose business last year topped the two million mark. It is our notion that Mr. Zevin might be just the baby we need to run the new Grosset & Dunlap for us, and if we don't get him, it won't be because I haven't exercised every wile at my command. I dragged him down with me yesterday to meet the assembled new bosses of G. & D., and he made a terrific impression. He is not the kind of guy you'd want to go away with on a long vacation but, for that matter, who'd want to go away with Hoyns either. Zevin is tough, hard-boiled, imaginative—and he's honest. Furthermore, he knows that chain store business inside out. He is really a dynamo. He is mixed up with his father-in-law out in Cleveland and I gather that both of them will be really delighted to get rid of each other. The old man can go back to his lucrative Bible and Dictionary business and get rid of his obstreperous young son-in-law, and the unneeded headaches of the reprint book business at one and the same time. At least, this is the way I dope it out, and it will be a great blow if I prove wrong. I am afraid Doc Lewis is irretrievably signed up with the Marshall Field interests and if both these guys are unavailable, we'll then have one hell of a time to find the right man to run the show for us. Of course, I will let you know the minute this angle is cleared up.

What we want most, of course, is to have you back on the job at the very earliest possible moment. You can see for yourself that even if we get Zevin our responsibilities are magnified ten times over. The future of the book business lies in the direction of mass markets and I feel that now we are right in on the ground floor, if we only know how to take advantage of our incredibly wonderful opportunity. Field and the Simon & Schuster gang will have to wait until paper is available to even start competing with us. By that time I hope we'll be so far out in front that we can watch their efforts, no matter how frantic, with complete equanimity. Lew Miller is, of course, seething with ideas for selling such literary gems as the Bobsy Twins and the Pollyanna books (which, it pains me to say, still sell about 30,000 apiece every year). Everybody else at Random House is also longing to get his finger into the pie. The fact remains, however, that we've got a full-time job in our own expanding business and you can't get back too soon to suit us. I hope that all this business at least convinces you of one thing: that there will be plenty of work for you to do when you get back to your desk!

Needless to say, when the news came out, there was such a buzzing around publishing circles as you've ever heard in your life. Other publishers want to come with us. The people that I thought were married to their jobs called up asking if we could find a place for them (examples, Ange from Doubleday, and Gene Armfield at P.W. Even old Charlie Boni crawled out of the woodwork somewhere to seek an editorial post.). This is only a beginning. Stan Griffis, on his way to Hawaii to become head of the Red Cross there, called up to say he'd like to finance the whole shebang. A half hour later Sam Goldsmith called to volunteer the same service, and incidentally to tell us if we didn't do it exactly in the way he suggested we were crazy as loons. The papers are running big stories and everybody looks upon the whole move as just the beginning of a knock down fight for post-war markets.

It is all terribly exciting, and my only regret is that you are not here to share it with us. Be sure of one thing, though, Don. We bought a magnificent business for little more than the quick asset value and if there is ever any chance of our being allowed to keep any profits in the post-war years, we are all going to be so God damned rich. . . .

Yippee. My deep love.

As ever,
Bennett

P.S.   I hope you will get a chance to tell our old pal Guinzburg about this deal and remember to describe his expression to me exactly when he hears the news.

P.P.S.   Sidney Satenstein and Van Cartmell must both be out of town. The news is now forty-eight hours old and I haven't heard a peep from either of these two babies. Imagine Sidney not being in on a big deal. They'll probably both pop up Monday morning.

P.P.P.S.   Do the General Headquarters know that you are anxious to get out when the German phase is completed? And can you hazard any guess whatever of how long thereafter it will take to have you scratching those what you may call it of yours in your old-time way in your old chair at 20 East 57th Street?

Oct. 14/44

Dear Bennett—

Received your letter of Oct. 2 to-day but I have not yet received Bob's letter giving details. It sounds so very exciting that I'm really heartbroken to have missed it.* I take it that a helluva lot of dough is involved but it looks pretty solid and substantial if old Stanton Gripps was willing to finance. I suppose the next thing we'll be doing is buying a printing plant and Brewtain's and then Thurman Arnold will be training his guns on us. Oh for the good old days of laissez faire capitalism! It really looks fine—and looks like lots of work for everyone involved— which is a good thing.

As for my return home—the over 38 deal is suspended over here for the present—but Jones knows that I want to go home after this is over— I've been turning down jobs right and left with that in mind. How long it will take me to get out of this and how many of us they'll let go is anybody's guess. Just tell me when the European war will be over and I'll make a guess. . . .

I flew down to Fighter Command yesterday to see Lynn. He has written a short history of the command which he wants me to read. He's applied to go home as the Fighter Command is being disbanded—he probably will get it in spite of this stoppage. I can't make up my mind whether the German opposition is holding us up on the western front or whether it's supplies that are doing it. Anyway the news is confusing but I think pretty good. We're still busy as beavers around here. The weather is our worst enemy.

---

*Pat Knopf, Alfred's son, unexpectedly witnessed Donald's excitement. Pat was the pilot of a B-24 bomber, and once had to make an emergency landing at an unfamiliar airfield with an engine out and a wounded tail gunner. As he climbed out of the plane he saw an officer peddling towards him on a bicycle. It was Donald. Both were surprised to see one another. After greetings were hollered, Donald asked Pat if he knew what just happened. Puzzled, Pat said he didn't. "We just bought Grosset!" Donald announced.

Give my love to Bob, Saxe—Pauline, Lew, etc. and I wish that I was home right now.

Love,
Donald

November 14, 1944

Dear Klops:

Your letter to Bob disclosing the fact that you had finally gotten the gory details of the Grosset deal arrived this morning and relieved all of our minds. We particularly loved your fervent declaration about getting home as soon as possible. All kidding aside, the closer supervision we can have of the Grosset layout in its early stages, the greater will be one, our influence in its future development, and two, the share of the spoils that we can legitimately claim for ourselves. You're right when you say that we have given up all but a very small stake of the company, but don't forget that we are the management and if we do our share of the job properly, we ought to cash in enough to make Bob's cousin, Henry Morgenthau, literally double up with laughter.

John O'Connor, our new Prexy [of Grosset], is the kind of a guy you like a little better every time you see him. Phyllis, Lew Miller and I took him out to dinner at the Stork Club the other night, where he promptly drank us all under the table. The evening had a funny conclusion. We poured O'Connor into the train for Chicago and started to wander home. We were standing in front of a Liggett window counting the number of copies there of a reprint edition of A TREE GROWS IN BROOKLYN when we heard a husky voice behind us inquiring, "What do you want to make of it?" Wheeling about, we discovered none other than Mr. Cass Canfield in his dinner coat and black fedora perched precariously on one ear and in a state considerably further to starboard than our own. It developed that he had just been to a dinner for the Swedish Commercial attache and was exuding schnapps at every pore. To make a long story short, he piled into a taxi with us and we came home to 62nd Street, where Cass stretched out until 3:30 A.M. telling us the complete and detailed story of his life. He is really a swell guy when he unbends, and the net result of the evening was a new sense of intimacy between us that I think is all to the good.

Our Random House activities are practically finished for the year since, as you know, we are fresh out of paper. PEOPLE ON OUR SIDE is romping along like a bat out of hell and will surely hit the 35,000 that we allotted it in our budget. It may even go a little further before January 1st. The two art books—THE FRENCH IMPRESSIONISTS and the National Gallery collection—turned out to be knockouts and we could have sold five times as many as we had of each of them. I think we'll be able to get a reprint of about 20,000 of the National Gallery book for next year. It really makes the Simon & Schuster TREASURY OF ART MASTERPIECES look like one of Whitman's Komiks for the ten-cent store. The Taylor cartoons is also a complete sell-out from the date of publication. Chris Massie's THE LOVE LETTERS and Allan Chase's FIVE ARROWS are both above 7000 and the first one in particular is a cinch to cross 10,000.

All in all, the Fall list was a smash success for us and, on the whole, added prestige to the line. Did I ever tell you that Harold Williams of the News Company disclosed the fact some time ago that Random House would be either fifth or sixth in total volume for the News Company this year. We also learned from KMV that our business is now greater than that of Knopf and Viking put together. When you consider the fact, Klopfer, that we are still only boy publishers, just think where we'll get when and if you ever reach puberty. That's a pretty dazzling thought. Take it slowly.

The great Cerf opus, TRY AND STOP ME, was published on November 3rd by those sterling fellows, Simon & Schuster, and if you think I haven't been getting a terrific bang out of the reviews, window displays and what not, you're crazy. They had the chutzpah to price the book at $3.00, although it was originally intended to be a Pocket Book of Anecdotes and, this being the kind of a year when people will pay anything for a laugh, will evidently cash in beyond my wildest dreams. The advance sale is 40,300 and the first week's reorders added 2800 more. The first printing is 50,000 and there are 25,000 more on press. I have a hunch that will just about end the party, but even so it is a bonanza. So far there has been only one unpleasant repercussion. Jezebel has now gotten so stuck up that she now considers that fanny of hers more sacred than ever, and even so experienced a manipulator as myself can't get near the measly little thing with a ten-foot pole. All is not lost, however. Several very likely prospects are developing in the Bookkeeping Department.

I am going to Cleveland tonight to address the Adclub there and do one of those idiotic book signing stunts for Halle Bros. I will repeat the performance for Marshall Field on Saturday and then I will come back to New York, probably a sadder and wiser man. At Fields I am following the luscious dame who wrote FOREVER AMBER (Macmillan's new and dirty successor to GONE WITH THE WIND), and that's going to be a tough spot because I understand she laid 'em in the aisles. I always preferred 112 West 59th Street (remember?).

. . .

There's been some bad news mixed up with the good. Red Lewis got word today that his son Wells had been killed in action. Ed McNamara, Ross' Irish pal, died last week. Clare Luce got reelected in Connecticut. On the whole, however, the election news was so wonderful and events at Random House have moved so smoothly that we are all happy as larks. Now if we can only get you back. . . .

My deep love,
Bennett

P.S.   I almost forgot to tell you we sold another Book-of-the-Month Club dividend. It is GREEN MANSIONS, with Ted Kauffer's wonderful pictures. That will start our new fiscal year with a bang. This is the second time we cashed in this way with an Illustrated Modern Library project and I understand that Confucius will be picked before many months more have gone by. This whole project is beginning to pay big dividends sooner than we ever dreamed it would!

Dec. 1, 1944

Dear Bennett—

I received my copy of your book and read it thru' in two sittings. It's really a damned good job—my heartiest congratulations. As a publisher I'd have liked to publish it and I think the public reaction to it will be grand. It should sell as many copies as S & S will allot it paper. You'll be so rich that you won't know what to do with your money. But, better than that, I think the book is really good.

I'm afraid you will have lost your bet on my being back at my desk Jan 1, 45—if the war ended to-day I wouldn't make it. I don't remember the stakes—it was either $25 or $100—you wrote it down in your book and I'd gladly pay the 100 to be back at my desk again. Don't let anyone ever tell you that this war business is anything but the most uncomfortable bore that you could possibly imagine. The whole 8th AF is bored—the thing has become so routine that there's very little creative work in it any more. But we still put out these enormous forces whenever the weather allows and we're doing some damage to Germany and they're knocking down some of our planes each time. The odds, I believe, are strongly in our favor. You proba-bly know more about the ground situation than I do—since the N.Y. Times does a better Intelligence job than any A2 section in the army.

Life around here goes on in much the same way. The crews come and go—the staff changes a bit—the Base remains the same. I assure you I envy you being with your wife and child and being in business about which you know something. It will be a great relief when that happens to me. Give the good Thrup and Chris a big Christmas kiss for me—on this side presents are unavailable so you'll have to forget this Xmas—and again, my congratulations on "Try and Stop Me."

My best to all at the office—

Love,
Donald

P.S.   Why always credit the corniest stories to me?*

DSK

*Bennett often used a character named Farmer Klopfer.

December 5, 1944

Dear Don:

In the first place, this letter is supposed to be my Christmas and New Year greeting to you. All of us seem to miss you around here a little bit more every day and you are going to get a reception when you finally come back that I think will sweep you off your feet. . . .

Enough of this Horatio Nostalgia stuff. I am enclosing herewith a tentative copy of our Spring publication schedule. It is slightly terrific and we won't have to add another item for the whole year to make it a sure-fire winner. I hope you will approve—as far as you are able to judge at that distance, anyhow. A couple of the items you won't recognize are sheer gambles on writers that may turn into something later on. We are lining up a lot of those right now by giving $250.00 apiece for options. I should say we've about ten such prospects in the bag. If only one of them comes through . . .

We have finally cleared the way on the Grosset deal and are about ready to do some concentrated master-minding on bringing the list up to date. Everybody is counting on you to play a big part in the picture when you come back. That's about the most challenging task imaginable and I only wish I could give more time to it. They are really living in the dark ages down at Grosset and the amount of work to be done is prodigious. I think we've got a swell guy in O'Connor. What we need most now is (one) a crackerjack manufacturing man, (two), a big league juvenile editor. Peggy Byrnes has hinted very broadly that she'd like the latter job. I don't know whether she is equal to it and I'd certainly hate to see her leave Macy's, but I know you will agree that we owe it to her to consider her claims very carefully. I am going to have lunch with her one day next week and talk it over. I will try to stall her until you come home. I will report on this later.

Speaking of Peg Byrnes, I went down to Macy's this morning at 9 o'clock and talked to the girls there about my own opus, TRY AND STOP ME. I explained that if you had been in this country, I wouldn't have been allowed within four blocks of the store but, under the circumstances, had managed to sneak in the salesmen's entrance. Peg has used 1500 copies of the book to date. The whole countrywide sale has been absolutely fantastic. In exactly one month, the poor thing has sold 65,000 copies. They've got another 25,000 on press and paper ordered for 25,000 more. All this for a book of corny jokes at the modest price of $3.00 per! It's too ridiculous for words.

Phyllis had done such a good job at 99 Park that they've made her a director. Dorothy Lee got married to Donald Hirsch (the guy who once was the husband of Betsy Smith). Georgie Opp has gone back to Hollywood. The Burma picture that he is working on will keep him there another two months, he hopes. He thinks by that time he may be able to get out of the Army altogether.

Reynal & Hitchcock are going to be the managers of a new book club that the C.I.O. is starting in January. It is to be called The Labor Book Club and will give six books a year for five bucks. The first two books are A BELL FOR ADANO and Howard Fast's FREEDOM ROAD. It sounds like a swell idea to me. I am trying to get them to use Allen Chase's FIVE AR-ROWS.

The whole Random House business goes along smoothly and there is certainly no sense in boring you with all the details. I think, however, you'd get a laugh out of all the sales we are making to 25¢ reprint houses on lousy old detective stories that sold 2200 copies five years ago and were then forgotten—stuff like DR. TOBY FINDS MURDER, and other turkeys whose names I can't even remember. It is all a sort of Alice in Wonderland, of course, with huge sums rolling in one door and out to the Treasury Department at the other, but it is kind of fun if you keep your perspective. One of the big things that we are getting out of this whole era of madness is the Illustrated Modern Library, which is so God damn beautiful and has such possibilities for the future that words temporarily fail me on the subject. And when words temporarily fail the Great Cerf, it is time to call a halt.

Get that job finished with, Klopfer, my fine buckaroo, and get the hell back here where you belong.

My love,
Bennett

Dec. 23—44

Dear Bennett:

Your long and welcome letter of Nov. 14th arrived to-day with a big load of mail from the States. The first I'd received in a couple of weeks. Believe me it was particularly welcome these days. I agree with you 100% as to my getting home as soon as possible. Don't misunderstand, Bennett, I hate it over here. I hate the Base. I detest England in the winter and I dislike the whole Army setup. The only saving grace is that the boys with whom I work are a really fine bunch of youngsters. But I feel so mentally stultified in this atmosphere that a normal boring evening with your Aunt Minnie would seem like the stimulation of Herbert Swope, Kip Fadiman and H.A. Wise! Nonetheless there's a job to be done and until my CO decides I am no longer of much use to the Group or the European war ends there is nothing that I can do to get out of it. I feel that I'm useless around here. He doesn't agree. So I'll grin and stick it out and try not to get any more involved than I am at present.

I'm mighty pleased with the reception Try and Stop Me is getting. You must be one worn out author what with autographing parties and literary teas. If Forever Amber is as dirty as they say it is please send me a copy. I'm a sex starved old man!

Of course the big news over here is von Rundstedt's drive.* He obviously caught our boys with their pants down and, altho' he's slowed down a bit to-day, he's by no means stopped. It was well done weatherwise—we've been grounded all week, chafing at the bit and fogged in so that even the birds are down. To-morrow the weather will break and we should be of some help. To-day we managed to struggle over and back but weren't too effective. Maybe the fighters did some good! Anyway, the next few weeks should tell how long the damned thing will last. I hope it's their last flying and they lose every damned German involved!

It looks as if we'll be really working Christmas day— I'll bet you're having a fine tree for Chris! Give my love to Thrup and the youngster—and to all the people at the office, the two Bobs, Pauline, Saxe, Harry and all!

Lots of love,
Donald

*The Battle of the Bulge.

1945

January 4, 1945

Dear Klopf:

I don't remember how much we bet on your being back at your desk by the beginning of 1945, but there is no question about my having lost, and I will settle with the greatest reluctance when you do show up here. I certainly was wrong in my calculations. From the way things look at this very moment, there is no telling either how wrong I was. I do want you to believe that the lengthening of your absence doesn't mean you are being missed any less here. All of us are simply snowed under with work these days, and I think somebody says, at least five times a day, "If that blankety blank Klopfer were only back here."

I hope it will please you to know that you were toasted on New Year's Eve by myself and none other than Donald Nelson and his beautiful bim. We all were at a big party at the Barberry Room and Jim Moriarty called me over to meet Nelson. The latter poured champagne for all of us and said, "Whom will we toast?" I suggested you and we all hoisted a couple to your good health and continued well-being. . . .

There is only one book on the Random House list this January, and that is the two Elliot Paul minor mystery stories chucked into one. We'll really get going in February, however, with as powerful and impressive a list as we've ever had. Catalogues are on press now and you will have one in a few days' time.

. . .

As far as my own personal activities are concerned, TRY AND STOP ME is over 80,000 and the printings are up to 120,000. Reader's Digest is taking about four pages from it for February, Omnibook in March, Liberty in April, and Scope in May. Jezebel and I consider that very fair coverage. Our next activity will be a joke book for the Pocket Book series which will consist principally of all the bum old gags that were left out of TRY AND STOP ME. Grosset needs a joke book very badly too, and we are trying to work up a deal whereby the book can be done for a quarter at Pocket Books and 49¢ at Grosset & Dunlap. The sale for these kinds of books these days is almost unbelievable and anything goes as long as people think they may get a chuckle or two out of it.

We have started the revamping of Grosset & Dunlap. I have asked Jez to send you a copy of the first new Grosset & Dunlap catalogues along with a copy of the last old one, so that you can see the difference for yourself. The first big change we are making is to change the name of the Madison Square series to Pinnacle Books and reducing the price from 50¢ to 49¢ to meet the competition. For the trade mark we have a circle with a mountain top enclosed—something like the Paramount Picture symbol. The next step will be to start a special motion picture department for special tie-ups with the picture companies. I think we are going to get Bernie Geiss, who has been the editor of Coronet and assistant editor of Esquire for the past five years, to come with us and head this department as well as acting as assistant editor in general. He is all lined up and the salary has been agreed upon at $15,000, but the move has to be approved by the Board of Directors' meeting next week. I have little doubt that it will be. Cass Canfield told us yesterday that he is going to Paris for six months to head the OWI there, so we'll have Henry Hoyns to contend with while he is gone. Maybe you will run into Cass while he is there. He is really a very swell guy and I like him better every time I see him.

If you ever get down to London any more, it occurs to me that you might do a little snooping down there along the following lines:

1. How hard and fast is the agreement between Dent and Dutton's on Everyman's. It might not do any harm to visit Dent and see what chance there may be of taking over the whole Everyman Series when the war is over and we can once more get all the paper we want. This is a possibility that I think is at least worth exploring.

2. It has always seemed to me that we ought to have some good English house with whom we had a first refusal exchange basis, something like the one between Harper's and Jamie Hamilton. Faber & Faber might be good for us, or Chatto & Windus or even Collins. Nobody would be bound to anything; it would simply be a gentleman's agreement whereby both firms gave the other first refusal in their respective countries on anything that wasn't already tied up by previous contract. Don't you think this is at least worth looking into if you get the chance?

3. No new English writer of the stature of Aldous Huxley or Maugham has popped up his head in the whole war as far as America is concerned. Don't you hear any rumblings about a new white hope over there? If so, couldn't we get our mitts on him for the far future? It might be a good idea to snoop around Pollinger's, Heath's, and that old such and such Watt to see if anything is cooking.

4. Here's something else you might look into while you are at Watt's. As you may remember, we have been trying for years

to do a Sherlock Holmes volume in the Modern Library. Our notion this summer was to do the Adventures of Sherlock Holmes and the Memoirs of Sherlock Holmes, i.e., the first two books of the Collected Stories of Holmes, and make one Modern Library volume of them. We thought we'd do it both as a regular Modern Library and as an Illustrated. We offered Harper's a $2500.00 advance against a 10¢ a copy royalty. This suited them fine, but Watt tried to put in a three-year limitation clause. This is, of course, ridiculous, since we'll have to make our own plates for the book and we cannot possibly come out under any time limitation clause whatever. Maybe you could use that old world charm of yours to convince them to let us have the property on a straight 10¢ royalty, with the $2500.00 advance, of course, and no time limit whatever. A lot of the stuff is out of copyright anyhow, but we couldn't proceed on this property now even if we wanted to because of the Harper complication. Put this proposition over, Klopfer, and we'll put an extra candle in the window for you until you come back.

This is about all except to wish you a happy birthday, since I don't suppose this letter will reach you much before that time. Write soon, and know that even if you have just the same old story of operations to tell us, it always gives everybody in the office deep pleasure to see that Gertrude Stein–like handwriting of yours on an envelope.

My love to you.

As ever,
Bennett

Jan. 10–45

Dear Bennett—

Just received your letter of Dec. 5—things are incredibly slow in coming thru' these days but I do seem to get letters eventually. The Spring list looks fine altho' there are lots of names cropping up on our lists that I no longer recognize. Nothing makes me feel so far away from RH as that one thing. When you have been used to being in on the birth of every-thing it's quite a shock to see the finished article being an-nounced without the usual pangs of birth preceding it. I do hope the Walter Clark book is a good one. He's potentially so damned good that I'd hate to see him flub up on his second opus. Your cheering words about the Illus. ML make my mouth water.

Peg's a grand gal, a good executive and a good merchandiser but I don't know how good a juvenile editor she'd be. That's a pretty specialized field and G & D are going to need an expert. On the other hand she would have the merchandising ap-proach to the show and that's what you want.

What are you doing with old #4 Rabelais—I see O'Henry's replacing it? It's good to see Nevins & Commager in the M.L.

There is no gossip around here—the guessers as to the end of the war have quit guessing and are now settling down to try to win the thing—I haven't any idea when I'll get home but I suspect it won't be until late this year at the earliest. I can't see any immediate end to this thing—on the other hand I don't see how the Germans can stand the pressure. . . . At any rate you can rest assured I'll be home at the earliest possible moment.

My very best to all at the office. I just received your joint Xmas card for which all thanks. Lots of love.

Donald

January 18, 1945

Dear Klopf:

I was particularly pleased to get your letter of December 23rd yesterday because I am sure fully four weeks have gone by since I last heard from you.

I must say it was a bit of a shock to have you asking for a copy of FOREVER AMBER, which was described only last night as the kind of book that a boy of fourteen reads with one hand. The book is going out to you under separate cover at once, although I am sure you are going to find that it is tenth rate trash. Alternate titles that have been suggested for it are FOREVER UNDER, THE UNROBED, TROLLOP WITH A WALLOP, and THE DAME WHO UNSHIFTED FOR HERSELF. Your literary tastes, Klopfer, are now lower than Haas's, and it's lucky for both of you that you still have one partner (myself) who reads a couple of chapters from Ptolemy every night before he goes to bed.

As though your request for FOREVER AMBER wasn't enough for one day, a note appeared in the paper that your cousin Wildberg was giving a lecture last night at Columbia University on the future of the drama in America. Even the fall of Warsaw scarcely restored my equilibrium.

The Spring list is already on its way to you. It's short in quantity but high in quality. The really amazing title on it is the Aquinas. It now becomes obvious that we could have sold 50,000 sets of this work this Spring if we had had the paper with which to splurge. Even so, it will be supporting you in your old age, which will be along any minute now.

In about another hour, I am having a conference with Beatrice Lillie and her agent, and hope before another 24 hours have gone by to have her signed to do a book for us on the story of her life. If this doesn't warrant an advance printing of 50,000 copies according to present market standards, I am the Wildberg of the publishing business—and I will ask for no cracks from you either on the subject.

TRY AND STOP ME has now reached the 88,000 mark, Jez has gained a pound and a half where she needed it most (and it's not for you either, it's for me), Haas's Colonelcy came through yesterday, the streets are covered with about four feet of snow, ice and slush, and I wish to hell you were back home. I am in such a good humor these days that I broke down completely last night and invited Sally Benson up to the house for dinner. I will be taking that blankety blank Fineman out yet, if this era of good will keeps up.

My deep love to you.

As ever,
Bennett

Feb. 7–45

Dear Bennett:

My request for Forever Amber, you dope, was for my cellmates who feel the need of sexual stimulus these days. We're all restricted to the Base for having the highest VD rate in the Division—not guilty! That's what happens on this island.

The RH list arrived and looks small but good. These days of allotting books will come to an end and then I'll have to rely on Aquinas to support me, which, I suspect the good Saint will do only too gladly because of my virtue. Is the City of Trembling Leaves good? I hope so—he's my white hope as a RH novelist.

The cracks are beginning to show in the German front now—with Komies across the Oder it should not take too long to end this damned mess—here's hoping it happens by the time you receive this. I'm more anxious to get home than you are to have me there.

Good luck and lots of love,

Donald

February 23, 1945

Dear Don:

Just a line to you before I head southward for two weeks of rest that I really need. The whole family sort of cracked up at the same time. Chris couldn't get rid of the croup and Phyllis had been overdoing it dreadfully at 99 Park. I packed them down to Miami early in the week and Lew and I are following tomorrow afternoon. Saxe will fly down on Sunday. We'll all have two weeks to sort of catch up with ourselves. Life has really been terribly hectic around here and, although it's fun, I think it is wise for all of us to stop and take a little breath. I only wish to hell you could be there with us. Don't think I do not realize that you have earned and probably need a vacation more than all the rest of us put together. Your turn will come, I hope.

The only other news I can give you at the moment is that, at a dinner at Sherwood's last night, I had for a dinner partner a young lady whose name I did not catch. After ten minutes I whispered to Neysa on my right and asked, "Who's the dame

I'm sitting next to?" Neysa shrieked with laughter and informed me that it was none other than your dream girl, Greta Garbo. She thereupon made me feel wonderful by telling the whole table about it. Garbo didn't seem to mind. In fact, she didn't talk to me for the rest of the evening.

I hope to find time to write you from Miami. Anyhow, you'll know we're thinking of you.

My deep love,

As ever,
Bennett

March 17–45

Dear Bennett:

I haven't heard from you in ages, but that is undoubtedly due to the mails which have been so bad that you can't keep up any kind of a correspondence. Besides which the only things of interest that I can relate are in the N.Y. papers the day after they happen over here. Only I'd be court martialed if I wrote what the papers published. We get lots of laughs out of the whole security problem over here.

They've just given three big blasts on the mortar which means there are some German bombers within a few miles of us. That is really the most futile sort of thing our few airplanes come over—drop their bombs—make a pass at a field and beat it for home—very much relieved I'm sure—and they do no appreciable damage. We just fill the holes up a little higher and go back to sleep. You can't help but compare that with a thousand bombers carrying a real load over a real target. We're out every day now—the weather has been pretty kind to us—and the destruction in Germany has been terrific. They'll never be able to say they didn't feel this war in the Vaterland. PRU coverage of targets that the RAF and 8th hit is startling at times and the analysis of captured targets points to more damage than we could see in the pictures. Now that the British have that 2200 lb bomb they can do even more destruction. What a war for civilized people to spend the time, energy and brains!

I'm in fine shape and very fed up with this whole show, but it's not so bad now that we're busy and have the feeling that it's the final round for this theatre. Here's hoping I can get home soon and back to work again.

And you know that you're a famous guy and get asked for your autograph, how's it with you—and Thrup and Chris? Are you happy? I hope you had a good time in Florida. I can't tell you how much I miss you and all of Random House.

Love,

Donald

March 27, 1945

Dear Klopf:

The Random House caravan is 100% back on the job. We all had a fine rest and Saxe in particular has never looked so well or seemed so carefree in his entire life. When you get out of your show, I think you ought to take about two months of just lying on your can in the sun, relax gradually, and completely recover your equilibrium. We've done without you this long and we'll manage to do a little longer. I guess I am following here the Pat Klopfer propaganda line—surely the first and probably the last time in my life—but I really think the gal has got something and that you owe it both to yourself and to her to take one whopping vacation before you even look at the multitude of jobs that you will find yourself plunged into the minute you get back into harness here. Personally, I can hardly wait to see that repulsive puss of yours leering at me again from across the desk, not to mention sticking your hand into places where it doesn't belong. (Jezebel refuses to amplify this statement.)

Everything at Random House proceeded smoothly as hell while we were away. Even the detective standbys like Eberhart, Disney, etc. have doubled in sales in the last few years, and drek that used to sell five or six thousand now sells twelve to fifteen without the slightest effort on our parts. I hope you like the new format of the detective stories. I think it is infinitely more attractive than the old and bulkier form. In fact, these wartime restrictions have succeeded in making the format of all books infinitely more satisfactory than they ever were before and I hope all the publishers will have sense enough to stick to this smaller format long after the actual necessity therefor has passed.

The Gertrude Stein book got wonderful reviews, including the front page in the Times Book Review, and we'll sell out our full two printings of 14,000. That's more than her 1st five books together did! Margaret Millar's THE IRON GATES is tops in its line and I think we'll be able to run that up to between 15,000 and 20,000 too. The two big question marks on the Spring list are the Walter Clark and the George Stewart. I won't rest until I see the leading reviews on both these books, which will be made or broken by what the leading critics say. We'll have substantial advances on both of them because of the authors' reputation and, come what may, they are fine books to have on the list.

. . .

For the Fall, of course, we are trying to save as much paper as we possibly can for Red Lewis's book which, as I think I have told you, is the best thing he's done in many, many years. Then we've got a short novel by Dick Tregaskis and Quent Reynolds is hard at work on a book that can possibly turn into a runaway. It is a story of a captain of the gunboat Wake which used to ply up and down the Yangtze River. The captain was taken prisoner by the Japs, escaped, was recaptured again, sentenced to death, and made a second escape on the very eve of his execution. It's real ten, twenty, thirty stuff and will be done in the "as told to Quentin Reynolds" manner that we used for THIRTY SECONDS OVER TOKYO.

I am sure Pat has kept you up to date on personal items such as the death of Merrill Wyler and of Walter Wanger's peculiar sister. Chick Satorius finally up and married that young Wave lieutenant he's been buzzing around with for the past couple of years. Mike Breslauer's mother died suddenly in Palm Beach. . . . Poor Mike has been having one hell of a winter of it. He came over to the house yesterday with his daughter Betty who is developing into a stunning-looking brat who, I understand, is causing havoc among the younger males in the community. One of her boys is Tommy Guinzburg. At present, he is fighting on Iwo Jima. (Jesus, did *that* make me feel old!)

TRY AND STOP ME is still rolling along at about 7000 copies a week. It's over the 135,000 mark now and its distribution by the Book-of-the-Month Club as the next dividend won't hurt either. Unfortunately, Simon & Schuster will soon have to drop it because of the paper situation but, by that time, it will be around 180,000 and then Van Cartmell wants to do it at $1.40. I still think this would have been an excellent book at the original 25¢ price that was intended for it. . . .

. . .

The next great piece of literature to bear the name of Cerf will be the Pocket Book of Jokes. Copies should be off press in a couple of weeks and I will rush you a few. If you think the stories in TRY AND STOP ME were corny and old, wait until you get a gander at this new lot. The newest one was pulled on the opening day of Queen Victoria's Diamond Jubilee.

The war news is almost too wonderful to be true and I feel in my bones that Klopferless days at Random House are rapidly drawing to an end. By me that's perfect!

Love and kisses from me and a provocative wiggle from that magnificent creature who is typing this note.

As ever,
Bennett

March 30—45

Dear Bennett—

Just received your letter of the 23rd of Feb—that took a long time to get here. You've gotten back from the good Florida vacation now and I'm sure all of you are much better. When I get back I want to take one myself. It's not that I'm working too hard or anything like that. It's the fact that there is no break in the week—each day is like the other and I've had almost 18 months of this overseas stuff now. I'm extremely healthy—yet I want to get off somewhere with Pat and learn how to live a civilized life. . . . I'm the only one in my whole section who has never spent a day in the hospital or missed a day of work. So I don't really mind it—but I want a change. I assure you it's much worse when we don't work steadily—that's the only saving grace—the work. I'll really be loaded for bear when I get back to Random House—that is if any one is any good after three years in the Army!

The war news is wonderful—we won't be of use around here much longer—then I'm crossing my fingers to get sent home. . . .

Donald

April 27, 1945

Dear Don:

Congratulations on the Presidential citation. I have a horrible feeling that by the time you come home you will be covered with so many medals and ribbons that you will look like a table of smorgasbord in a Swedish restaurant. My only hope is that this won't give you an unfair advantage with Jezebel who, in her half-witted way, is always ready to swoon at the sight of anything in uniform from Bobby Heller to the doorman at the Roxy Theatre. Incidentally, Bobby Heller is getting out of uniform on Monday and I figure that if Heller comes, can Klopfer be far behind? The official announcement today that the Russian and Allied troops have joined up, coupled with all the other news from Germany, would seem to indicate that the end cannot be far off no matter what those fanatical Nazi idiots may still have up their sleeves.

Both Random House and Grosset are running smoothly and I have only gotten hell from Bob for interrupting him three times in the past twenty-four hours; MGM has bought Red Lewis's new novel for 150,000 bucks (Random House's share, nix); and Ed Snow has delivered another swell book to us for Fall publication. We are going to call it THE PATTERN OF SOVIET POWER. Sweet jumping Jesus, what a list we are going to have this Fall. Better come home quickly, my boy, and help us worry about where in hell we are going to get the paper for it.

My deep love to you.

As ever,
Bennett

P.S.   Try as we will, that magnificent and lengthy feud between your distinguished bride and myself seems to be degenerating into a beautiful love. This may be one more reason why you'd better hurry home. Also, Eddie Rosenwald is sore at me for neglecting him. You will be able to fix that up too, I know.

May 6–45

It's all over but the shouting as far as this theatre is concerned but how long I'll have to sit on my ass around here, I don't know. It's mighty deadly—we haven't flown in ten days or more and we'll soon start the big educational program if we get permanently stood down. That will be ducky!

The gov't ought to give us paper to manufacture ML books for the forces in the east. Boy, they'll need it!

Enclosed herewith a picture of RH's contribution to the war effort!

Love,
Donald

May 18, 1945

Dear Don:

God knows where you are at the moment and whether this letter will ever reach you, but anyhow. . . .

1. Heartfelt congratulations on the Croix-de-guerre and all the other little doodads you've acquired. Everybody in the office is really so proud of you that we are busting.

2. The Book of the Month Club has taken Red Lewis's CASS TIMBERLANE for their October selection. This is the first single choice we've had since you got out of diapers.

3. The Literary Guild has definitely accepted the Bedside Book of Great French Stories. The contract isn't signed yet, but it's in the bag.

4. For God's sake, hurry up and get home. Things are popping around here and you've had a long enough vacation.

My deep love,
Bennett

May 17–45

Dear Bennett:

Cancel all letters, books, etc. I'm probably sailing for home the beginning of June and should be in by July—unless things are changed before we get on the boat.

Love,
Donald

ABOUT THE TYPE

This book was set in Weiss, a typeface designed by a German artist, Emil Rudolf Weiss (1875–1942). The designs of the roman and italic were completed in 1928 and 1931, respectively. The Weiss types are rich, well balanced, and even in color, and they reflect the subtle skill of a fine calligrapher.